Why Not?

The Story of a City Girl
Who became a Cattle Rancher

By Ruth K. Raun

Why Not?
The Story of a City Girl
Who became a Cattle Rancher

By Ruth K. Raun

East of the Mountains and West of the Sun

RHYOLITE PRESS LLC
Colorado Springs, Colorado

© Copyright 2022 Ruth K. Raun. All Rights Reserved.

All Rights Reserved. No portion of this book may be reproduced in any form or by any electronic or mechanical means, including information storage and retrieval systems, without permission from the publisher, except by a reviewer who may quote brief passages in a review. Although this is a work of non-fiction, some proper names have been altered or substituted for privacy purposes.

Published in the United States of America by Rhyolite Press, LLC
P.O. Box 60144
Colorado Springs, Colorado 80960
www.rhyolitepress.com

Raun, Ruth K.

Why Not?
The Story of a City Girl
Who became a Cattle Rancher

1st printing, January, 2022

ISBN 978-1-943829-40-8
Library of Congress Control Number: 2021922514

Publisher's Cataloging-in-Publication data

Names: Raun, Ruth K., author.
Title: Why not? The story of a city girl who became a cattle rancher / Ruth K. Raun.
Description: Colorado Springs, CO: Rhyolite Press, 2022.
Identifiers: LCCN: 2012922514 | ISBN: 978-1943829-40-8
Subjects: LCSH Raun, Ruth K. | Ranch life--Colorado--Biography. | Colorado--Biography. | BISAC Biography & Autobiography / Women | BIOGRAPHY & AUTOBIOGRAPHY / Personal Memoirs
Classification: LCC CT274.R358 R38 2022 | DDC 978.8/092--dc23

PRINTED IN THE UNITED STATES OF AMERICA

Book design & layout by Suzanne Schorsch and Donald Kallaus
Cover design by Donald Kallaus

My grateful thanks to all of those who have been part of Eagles Nest Ranch: Beth Beattie whose persistent encouragement compelled me to write about my ranching experiences, My husband, Art, who encouraged and supported me in all aspects of this project, and my son, Greg, who along with Art helped me understand the technical details of cattle production. Also, Nancy and Vern VanVonderen who helped with many tasks, rode shotgun on trucking adventures and spent many evenings in the barn playing bridge while awaiting a new birth. Thank you so very much.

CONTENTS

Preface	1
Time Before Ranching	3
Naming the Ranch	23
The Barn, Our Working Home	29
Please Fence Me In!	45
When a Cow is not Just a Cow?	59
Who's Who in the Bovine World	69
The Miracle of New Life	75
Parting is Such Sweet Sorrow	85
Just Another Day	95
Tales about Tails	103
Calf Stories	111
On the Road Again	115
When the Sperm and the Egg Meet	139
Deere John	149
Stewards of the Land	159
If You Don't Like the Weather, Wait Five Minutes	171
Eagles Nest as a Nature Preserve	185
Sad Days and Glad Days	197
The Sharing of Ranch Life	199
So Why Not "Why Not?"	205

View from the window at Eagles Nest Ranch, looking west toward Pikes Peak.

PREFACE

After hearing stories at our annual Church School picnic about our cows and calves here on Eagles Nest Ranch, a dear friend, Beth Beattie, insisted I write a book. This was not a new idea as I had been thinking about this before, not necessarily a book to be published, but one for our grandchildren who loved coming to the ranch. Not only did Beth encourage me but so did my husband, Art, who even gave me time off from doing chores so I could write. With this writing I have answered all the questions asked by the picnic attendees over the past sixteen years.

This story is about me, what I had to learn about cows and what it takes to be successful ranchers. My mistakes on various new terms will provide the readers with either memories or laughs depending on the situation, but laughing is Ok because I laugh at myself. There was so much to learn and so many, many new experiences. It has been and continues to be a whole new way of life.

I have enjoyed writing this book and being able to share my experiences with others who have had or might never have this terrific opportunity to observe nature at its best. May it bring smiles to all faces.

TIME BEFORE RANCHING

This is a true story about how a city girl, me, Ruth and a country boy, Art, ended up on a cattle ranch in Colorado. It wasn't an overnight thing but took many years filled with the meeting of many interesting people and three different types of life styles. The purpose of this story is not to tell how I had to change my wardrobe from professional "garb" to a more practical one of jeans, boots, and a cowboy hat on special occasions, but to let other city folks walk a mile in my boots. When I get to the cattle ranching part of this story, for those of you who have already experienced events told in this saga, may it bring smiles to your face or even make you laugh out loud. For those of you who have never had the opportunity to learn about cattle raising, may it be a learning experience and you might say "Oh, my gosh. Is that really the way it is?"

This story begins when I met this good looking fellow, Art, who was working on his doctoral at Iowa State University in Ames, Iowa. I had gone to the campus for the Homecoming weekend to visit friends I knew from my year at ISU. Art was having coffee at my friend's apartment with other friends and I was invited to join in. When he told me he was from Nebraska, I said I thought the only way to see Nebraska was at night with your eyes closed. Apparently, he really had not heard what I said or maybe he just shrugged it off because about three weeks later, he called and asked me for a date. This meant him having to drive the one hundred miles from Ames to Cedar Rapids where I lived. I was happy that he thought enough of me that he would take the chance. The meeting went well and there were many more dates. Sometimes, I would take the train to Ames and other times, Art would drive the route.

There was so much to learn right from the first meeting. Art was using sheep as an experimental animal to study growth rates in ruminants. For me, I had to use the dictionary for the definition of a ruminant. A ruminant is a cud chewing animal with a very unique digestive system which involves them having four stomachs. As far as I was concerned, the sheep that I saw with Art were in cages and needed to be fed before putting me on the train and sending me back to Cedar Rapids. Since we had started dating in November, wool clothes were the necessity for the cold weather in Iowa. When I would get on the train, I felt I smelled like the sheep. This was OK because I usually got a seat all to myself. This was also OK because then I could get some sleep and be sort of ready to go back to my job as a secretary for Johnson Control Company the next morning. In July when we knew we would be getting married in September, Art gave me all his wool sweaters to wash. This involved many washes with Woolite to remove the smell left from the sheep. This truly was a challenge!

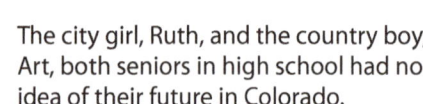

The city girl, Ruth, and the country boy, Art, both seniors in high school had no idea of their future in Colorado.

Art had been raised on a farm in Minden, Nebraska. He received a Bachelor Degree from the University of Nebraska but had decided to go on to graduate school because he really did not want to continue the family tradition of farming. He had been a member of the local 4-H and had shown steers at both the county and state fairs every year. He had received a Master's Degree from Iowa State and was working on his Ph.D. in Ruminant Nutrition. This proved to be quite important, not only for his future, yet unknown, employment at Eli Lilly and Company but also when we started raising cattle thirty-five years later. As a youngster on the farm, they had "feeder cattle" meaning cattle were purchased in the fall and fed out to be slaughtered. During the winter, these animals would be taken to stock yards in Omaha. Here buyers from various packing plants would bid on the animals which would then be taken to the various plants to become meat for the grocery stores. Children are often asked, "Do you know where your meat comes from?" The answer is always, "The grocery store." They know not otherwise.

I had so much to learn about animals and especially the ones Art was working with. Growing up the only animal my family and I had was a neutered cat. I had visited farms owned by friends of my parents but these were self-sustaining operations with chickens, dairy cows, hogs but not meat producing cattle. I did get to ride a horse a couple of times which was quite disastrous. I usually went down as the horse was coming up and I even got dumped off in a raspberry patch. It was then I decided the horses knew I really didn't like them which I think was mutual. I did get to see some piglets being born one time but I realize now, that was nothing compared to a cow giving birth. Later on in life, as a parent of two boys who had acquired a female cat, I did get to see the new born kittens but not the actual birthing process as she had gone off by herself as all cats do. So much for knowing about animals.

September came and our wedding date was fast approaching. Art knew he had to report for active duty in the Air Force but so far, no notice had been received. One day as I sat at my desk in the office, the phone rang. It was Art saying he had gotten his orders to report on September 14th. Our wedding was scheduled for the 20th. I just sat there, not saying a word but wondering what to do and how can I get everything changed. At last, Art said, "I'm kidding. I have to report on the 25th." At that moment, I think I might have killed him but maybe this was a sign of how the future would be. At this time, he was working for Pfizer in Terre Haute, Indiana, but would be back in Iowa for his graduation in August. Can't say we saw much of each other for that period of time but I was busy making my wedding dress and sending out invitations.

The day came. We were married in Central Park Presbyterian Church. We left immediately following the ceremony and reception for our new life together in Dayton, Ohio.

All of our earthly belongings were packed in the 1958 Chevy Impala white convertible, leaving behind wedding gifts to be delivered when we found housing. We left Iowa, driving through and stopping many times to do sightseeing though Wisconsin, the upper peninsula of Michigan, onward south to Dayton, home of the Wright Patterson Air Force Base. We were welcomed the first night with a dinner at the home of one of Art's friends from graduate school. The next morning, I pressed his uniform on the bed, as it was the only flat place available, other than the floor. That was before motels furnished ironing boards! Off to work went First Lieutenant Arthur P. Raun to the Aero-Medical laboratory where he would be doing nutrition research in support of the space program. He returned to the motel with a smile on his face and said, "We're really lucky. We have housing available." The next morning, we checked out of the motel and I went to what would be our home for the next three years–or so we thought!

Air Force Years

My first experience as an Air Force wife was a bit unnerving to say the least. The housing was what was called "Wherry Housing" which today would be town houses. It was a two story, two-bedroom, one bath, a kitchen and a great room! There was a window on the front in the living room, and a window in the back. Since we were in an end unit, there was also a window on the back side. Not much to write home about but we did have entertainment. Every time a B-47 or B-52 took off from Patterson field, they would fly over our unit. The noise was deafening but it meant America's finest were at work protecting each and every one of us. The neighbor's back door and our back door were side to side and when the neighbor realized a new person was moving in, she came over. She introduced herself and proceeded to tell me that the lady who had lived here before fell down the steps and broke her arm three times. That was not what I needed or wanted to hear but I soon realized, she was not a happy person. What made it even worse, was she would come over every day to see if I was properly dressed and if my dinner table was properly set for dinner. Oh well, it takes all kinds! Fortunately, the other neighbors took pity on us and brought in dishes, pans, utensils, lawn chairs and even lamps that we could use until we got our own things. This was taken care of quickly as we went shopping on the weekend at a store recommended by neighbors especially for military personnel. I always say, "The overhead there was so low, we had to duck to get through the door." We bought a couch, a bed, a chest of drawers, a table and chairs using the $500.00 Art's folks had given us as a wedding gift. The stove and refrigerator were already part of the kitchen. We had brought with us a coffee pot, an electric skillet and a couple of floor pillows. We were all set! A TV would come later as would all the wedding gifts as my mother had family in Nelsonville, Ohio, and Dayton was right on the way. The most important piece of furniture was a pole lamp. When summer appeared, so did the pole lamps with extension cords reaching from individual units so croquet games could be played in the center grassy area of the units. I am sure that those not participating in the games did not appreciate the enthusiasm as the games went on deep into the night. This was a special time in our lives as we were surrounded by couples all about the same age. No one had any extra money, so when one person made a dessert, it was made to serve all others. Sometimes, we would pool our change and get ingredients for homemade ice cream or pizza. It was a wonderful experience and friendships made there lasted for many years.

We spent eleven months at Wright Patterson with a month temporary duty yonder (TDY) in Oak Ridge, Tennessee, where Art was attending a short course on laboratory use of radioisotopes. We stayed in a cabin at Norris Dam and enjoyed sightseeing in the region. Within a month after returning from Oak Ridge, Art received a phone call asking if he would like to move to the Air Force Academy in Colorado where he would be teaching Human Physiology. Our supposed three years at Wright Patterson was now ended. Since I was pregnant with the baby due in December, it was decided we would stay at Wright Patterson until after the baby arrived. This changed quite suddenly! Art came home from work on Monday evening and said, "The packers will be on Wednesday, the movers will be here on Thursday and we will leave on Friday. I need to be in Colorado for the beginning of the fall semester." WOW! To leave military housing, everything must be SPOTLESS! If not, an outside cleaning team is used and the last occupants must pay for the job. Fortunately, there were just the two of us and we certainly hadn't acquired much in the ten months we had been living there, so we were good to go.

Before leaving our home in Dayton. a very exciting event happened for me. I had learned how to tell the various aircraft flying overhead by their sound. However, on this one afternoon, there was a very strange and unfamiliar sounding aircraft approaching my housing area. Of course, I was extremely curious so just had to go outside to see what plane it was. I looked up as it slowly approached my unit. I kept my eyes on it as it flew by and it was a plane I had never seen before. It was HUGE! It was flying so slowly or so it seemed and then it landed on Wright Field. When Art came home, I told him what I had seen. His remark was, "Draw me a picture." Well, he knew quite well that I could only draw stick figures so drawing a picture of an aircraft would be utterly impossible. "OK, how many propellers did you see?" Well, I think I saw six but they were backwards," I replied. "It was really a huge plane." This was not a whole lot of information to go on. "Was there anything else you noticed?" "There was something on the end of the wings. Does that help any?" Art being an airplane enthusiast, thought for a moment and said, "Maybe it was a B-36." Of course, that was exactly what it was. As it had landed on Wright Field, which was within walking distance of our house, we could look across to the airfield and we both could get a better look at this enormous aircraft. This proved to be a historical moment as this was not only the last flight for this particular craft but for all B-36's. The plane had parked exactly on the predestined spot and the Air Force Museum was built around it. Even after leaving Dayton, we have returned many times to go through the museum. On my last visit I looked into the bomb bay of this B-36. I'm not sure how many bombs it would hold but it was a huge area but hard to describe. The museum is terrific and certainly one worth visiting. I will never forget that afternoon when the B-36 flew over my head and I was witnessing history being made.

A few days later, we left our friends, vowing to keep in touch. This time we drove west from Ohio into Indiana along US highway 40, which then was a three-lane highway. We saw houses with steps so close to the road that I wondered if the occupants were even safe there. As we drove through Indiana, little did we know that in three years we would be living within walking distance of US 40. On across Illinois and back to Cedar Rapids where I would spend three weeks or more with my family, depending when the construction of our house at the Academy would be finished. After that time, I took the train to Minden and spent time with Art's family. The plan was that when the house was ready Art would come to Minden to get me. What an experience that was. I really didn't know Art's folks well but they trusted me enough to give me the keys to their car and send me off to the country to be with my sisters-in-law. This was great except I had only been to Minden a couple of times before. I was sure I would get lost and not know how to get back to town. The worst part was that I knew absolutely no one but Art's family and how embarrassing it would be, not only for me, but for the family if this new daughter-in-law had gotten herself lost.

The house was finished. Art came and got me. On the 27th of September we drove to Colorado and our new home on the base of the United States Air Force Academy. What an honor and privilege this was. On the highway as we entered Colorado Springs, there was a sign saying "Watch For Snow Plows." How can that be? It is only September. But it was true. That night we received thirty-six inches of snow. The power was intermittent, which meant so was the heating of our house. We stayed snug in the bed supplied by the Air Force, under the sheets and an old itchy Army blanket that Art's mother had given us. Our furniture was stranded in Colorado Springs and would be delayed. PERIOD! For how long was any one's guess. The morning saw Art go off to teach as the cadets could make it to class so no "Snow Days" here. I was left in our wonderful Capehart housing which was certainly an upgrade from that at Wright Patt. Only problem, the heat was not working and since Art had just received the keys to the house, there was no wood on hand for the fireplace. This time I met the neighbors before they even knew I was there to be "welcomed." I was cold, the oven in the kitchen did not put out much heat so I put on my winter coat (which fortunately had come with me) and walked to the neighbors. They opened the door and I said, "I am Ruth Raun. I got here last night and I am cold." Of course, the answer was "come in, have a seat by the fire and how about a cup of hot chocolate!" We became friends immediately. The furniture came a few days later and we settled into our new home where we thought we would live for two more years while Art continued his tour of duty.

Our new home had three bedrooms, one bath, a galley kitchen supplied with a gas stove, a refrigerator, and a dishwasher, which was new to me. There were large windows all along the west wall looking toward the Rampart Range. The east windows in the two bedrooms gave us a view of the (at that time) vacant land on the eastern plains. There were casement type windows in the third bedroom just perfect for the new baby when it arrived. We had a basement containing a washer and dryer which to me was an appliance sent from heaven as it meant no more trips to a laundromat. Everything that we needed had been supplied for us. This was GREAT! Everyone connected with the Academy was living on base either in Douglas Valley or Pine Valley where we were. This included enlisted personnel as well as officers of all ranks. There were different sizes of units depending on size of families and rank. It was like having a big family. We knew our neighbors but one thing lacking were the croquet games. We had a back yard and front yard but when we moved in, there was not a blade of grass to be found at either location. Eventually, there was a type of ground cover planted but when it grew, we were told to watch out for rattlesnakes. When the wind would blow, which was quite often, it was not unusual to find sand/dust on the windowsills. There were no trees but no one complained as we all knew; better things would be coming with time. The grass finally grew, as did flowers that we planted but none of us ever complained as we all thought we were definitely in God's Country.

For me being the wife of an officer at the most visited tourist attraction in Colorado, there were a few unwritten rules to be followed. One was, I was to be properly dressed at all times. The officers' wives were to set an example for the cadets as they prepared for married life. The dress code was strict to the point that Art had to be in full dress uniform when he took me to the hospital to have our baby. When we went to football games in Denver, (the stadium at U.S.A.F.A. was in the early construction stages) the women were to be dressed in hose, heels and gloves. I also learned that our quarters should be in tip top shape by 9 a.m. and should be ready for visitors should they appear at any time. This proved to be very true because that first year, we had seventy-five people show up at our door. One time, Art had come home for lunch and as we were finishing, I looked out the window and saw this man walking up our drive. He continued into the back yard but by that time, I had asked Art, "Who is that man walking up our drive?" It happened to be his dentist from Minden who he had not seen for many years. Apparently, Dr. Strand had gotten directions from Art's mother so he knew exactly how to get to our house. Usually, people would stop at either the North or South Gates of the Academy and ask for directions or would call from there to see if we were home. There was one time, when we had one set of friends leaving as the second set came in. A really quick change of sheets was made and the visitors did not realize what was being done and I'll never tell.

The visitors were always given a tour of the grounds. The hospital and Chapel were still under construction. They would always be treated to seeing the classrooms and laboratories. The classrooms were small as the average number of students in a class was fifteen at the most. The laboratories had the latest equipment and stainless-steel tables. The library was, to me, always a special place as one whole side wall was windows. There was a circular stairway going into the library that looked upon a wall of tiny red tiles, too many to count. It was also fun to watch the Cadets as they marched to the Dining Hall, or if they were freshmen (doolies) they would have to run. If they were met by an upper-class man, the doolie would have to stop, stand at attention and salute before continuing his run to the dining hall. At that time, 1959, there were 1,400 Cadets, less than one-third of the current enrollment. There were no "sponsors" but each officer was assigned five cadets who were given the opportunity to become part of the officers' family. The Cadets could be picked up after football games, or on weekends for dinner or for whatever the family might be doing. The Cadets did not have cars until they were seniors which explains the "picking up." We had girlfriends spend nights with us when they were on campus for a special event. This new life style was rather amusing as I was being addressed as "Ma'am" and the Cadets were only about two years younger than me, but that of course, is what the rule was for them. To this day, we have friends who were Cadets and they still address us as "Ma'am" or "Sir!" Old habits are hard to break.

On the private side of life, while at the Academy, one memorable experience was that of having a baby. As mentioned before, the hospital on base was not yet finished so an alternate had to be found. There was a hospital at Fort Carson, located on the south side of Colorado Springs so one day I drove down there to have a look. It was an old WWII vintage wood building, built many years before and after leaving a much more modern one at Wright Patterson, this was just not to do. I went home and told Art, "I am not going to go to that one." "OK, where will you go" was his comment. "I don't know, but it won't be there." After that day, I found there were three other women due to deliver all within a couple of months. They were basically neighbors as they lived in the same block of houses just across the street from me. We joined forces and drove to Fitzsimmons Army Hospital in Aurora (Denver) for our monthly visits. We would check in, get weighed, see the doctor and leave. Before driving the sixty miles back to the Academy, we would go to the dining room at Stapleton Airport for lunch and a piece of the best strawberry pie in the world. December came, the first woman delivered a beautiful baby boy. One week later, I delivered our baby boy, Tim, who weighed in at nine pounds, seven ounces. He was used as a model as other mothers and myself were given instructions on how to correctly bathe a new born. My doctor told me I was breaking all the rules as going anywhere sixty miles from the hospital was a "No, No." Oh well, I just had to do what I had to do and we made it home without any problems. When we got home, Art had already had the Christmas tree decorated so we put Tim under the tree and took his picture. That's what proud parents do! The other two women delivered their babies within the next couple of months but one did not quite make it to the hospital. Her husband delivered the beautiful baby girl in the backseat of their car but since he was an instructor of Human Physiology, he knew exactly what to do. The only problem was that when he checked in at the security gate of the hospital, he declared "mother and son." When he got to the office the next day and was telling his story, he said, "Well, from the back all babies look alike!" He never did live that down.

Some things I learned while at the Academy was how to can tomatoes and how to play bridge, but with only certain people because I was a terribly slow learner. Still am, for that matter! I learned how to decorate cakes. One of the other wives had taken lessons for cake decorating so she in turn taught others. Only problem, when baking cakes at that attitude, of 7000 ft., they didn't always come out as planned but of course, a lot of frosting could help the situation.

Art's two-year assignment turned into three years as the United States was dealing with the building of the Berlin Wall and all military personnel were to stay in place. This was fine as he had not really started looking for civilian employment. But in early June, Art got word that he was being relived from active duty. Our days at the United States Air Force Academy were over but would never been forgotten nor would all the friends we were leaving behind. There again, little did we know that in thirty-one years, we would be back in Colorado where we would be living close to the Academy and in touch with many of the friends we had left behind. Many of them had retired and moved back to Colorado Springs.

Kids, PTO and Scouting

It was early June of 1962 as we were leaving the military life and our many friends to become civilians. This time we were driving east on US 24 leaving behind the sign that read, "Watch for Snow Plows." The Rampart Range remained in our review mirror until turning east and heading for Nebraska. The route of three years prior was the same only in reverse and now we had a two-and-a-half-year-old asleep in the back seat of a much smaller car. Once again, I was pregnant and making numerous stops along the way, allowing Tim to get out and run a bit and me, to stretch my enlarging body. We spent a week in Nebraska with Art's family where Tim got acquainted with his cousins. He got to ride on Grandpa's tractor and have a "big orange" drink at Grandpa's shack. (Always a treat for the grandchildren.) After that we drove to Cedar Rapids where we were with my family. Here again, Tim got acquainted with Kim, his only cousin there. When they were together, I realized that "Tim" and "Kim" sounded a bit alike when they were called. One or the other would answer but not necessarily the one actually being called. At any rate, it was a fun week.

Leaving Iowa, we started our drive eastward to Greenfield, Indiana, where Art would be employed by Eli Lilly and Company. As mentioned before, we had driven through Greenfield on U.S. 40 as were heading west from Ohio. We had driven past the beautiful Spanish looking buildings on the grounds of the Lilly facilities. Art had known of this company due to his Ph.D. research at Iowa State but never did he dream he would be employed there. His job was to be that of discovering and developing products to improve the growth and efficiency of ruminants.

A rental house had been found for us. It was a small one but within walking distance of a laundromat and grocery store. This being important as we were a one car family with no washer or dryer. The neighbors were nice and very friendly but one thing I kept thinking was, "we are as far south we can be without actually being in the south." The people talked so slowly, I wanted to reach into their mouths and pull the words out. Within the first week in Greenfield, I learned when the "natives" spoke about Indianapolis, they would say, "We're going to the city" which was only about thirty miles away. After living in Colorado, thirty miles seemed like "next door!" The other thing I quickly learned was that a "Pot Luck" was now a "Pitch In" dinner as we were invited to a 4th of July picnic. Art's roommate, Jim Foster, while living in Ames, was from Greenfield and his family owned and operated a farm on the edge of town. Over the years, we became close friends and when I needed information on where to shop, I would call Mrs. Foster. They also supplied us with the best sweet corn and ripe tomatoes as only found in the Midwest.

We lived in that little house from the first of July until September 15th. I remember those dates well as Greg was born in the Hancock County Memorial Hospital on the 13th of September. On the following two days, fellow co-workers from Lilly helped Art move us into a larger house. His secretary, Esther Raymon and her daughter did the unpacking of boxes, made the beds and did everything she could to make it livable for me and our new baby. Only problem was that I would have to call the office and ask Esther where such and such might be. She always knew exactly where I should look. She was a much loved and appreciated super lady whom we will never forget. We would be renting this place from a Lilly employee who would be in Michigan working on his Ph.D. for three years. This would be just fine.

The first years in Indiana saw Art traveling, meeting co-workers in what was called "the field." Actually, they were doing providing technical service to cattle feed lots. The first spring had me terrified most of the time because of the many tornado warnings and sightings. There were only a few houses with basements so we were told to go into the bathroom, where there were many pipes in the walls, get into the bath tub and pull a mattress over our heads. SURE! How do you do that with any small children, let alone a babe in arms? One night, a neighbor who also had two small children, came to the door and said, "Grab what you need, such as a bottle, diapers, snacks, etc. We're going to drive away from the storm." Oh, my gosh! We had only seen one tornado in Colorado and it had been high in the foothills. I don't remember having tornadoes when I was a child. We did have bad storms but there again, there was no warning system as there is now. I kept thinking, "Why, oh why did we leave Colorado?" Of course, the answer was, "Indiana is where there is a job."

Three years later, in late August, we moved to our very first owned home which we had built in rural New Palestine where Tim would be starting kindergarten. Here we had four bedrooms, two baths, kitchen, living room with dining area in an L-shape formation and a family room with a fireplace. Best of all, we had walls of windows through which we could look out over fields of corn or soy beans. No hills and unfortunately, no mountains.

By this time, Greg was no longer a baby and Art was not traveling as much. Plus, I had gotten used to the tornadoes. Now the warnings came with the announcements of where the storm had been sighted and which direction it was heading. In addition to that, we now had neighbors down the road that had a basement in their "farm house" and were willing to share it with us.

Time went on, our neighborhood now consisted of eighteen homes on a cul-de-sac. The children occupying these homes were all about the same ages. The school bus stopped at every house or when nice, the students would walk a quarter of a mile to the main road. Art's work was about seven and half miles from home so our daily lives turned into a regular routine.

Breakfast for Art, then for the boys after which they would head out the front door for the bus. Now it just me and the calico cat, Sally, at home. Sometimes I would be embarrassed when asked if I worked outside the home. But then I realized my work and time spent as a mother was absolutely the best life in the world. As the boys grew, I became involved with their activities so I wasn't just a "stay at home" mom. I was a Room Mother when students were allowed to celebrate birthdays with their classmates. I tutored students when they needed assistance with reading. I helped out in the school library and was even PTO and Band Booster president at other times. Most of all, though, I was a Cub Scout Den Leader and always had snacks waiting as the boys got off the school bus at our house for Den meetings. Art served as a Scout Commissioner and when Tim moved into Webelos, Art was his leader. When Tim moved into Scouts, Art became the Scout Master. When Greg joined the Scout Troop, I gave up the Cubs but became a Den Leader Coach for other mothers. I would work with them, sharing project ideas for the Blue and Gold banquets and for the exhibits at the annual Scout Fair. I also would share my experiences and express to them how all the money in the world could not pay them for the opportunities they were giving these young boys. For Art and me, we will never forget the boys who we watched grow into manhood. We really enjoyed seeing our boys, not only our sons, but also those from along the way when they stood on stage to receive their Eagle Rank.

Our sons graduated from New Palestine High School and went on to graduate from Purdue University. While Greg was finishing at Purdue, I decided I would like to get a college degree as I was the only one in the family without one.

I had worked as a church secretary but now at age fifty, I would attend Indiana University Purdue University at Indianapolis. (IUPUI) as a returning student. I began by just taking classes that sounded interesting to me. The first class was on Indiana Folk Lore. Not being from Indiana, I found this to be a bit of history. One of my classmates was a lady who was eighty-five years of age. When asked why she was taking classes, she said she did not want to become "brain dead." OK, if she can do it, so can I. After two years of taking only one class a semester, I realized I was making good grades and should think seriously about becoming a real student. Speaking with advisors, it was decided I would major in Geography with a minor in American History. Readers must realize this all took place before the decision was made to raise cattle! So, the question I receive most is, "Did you ever use your degree?" Yes, the Meteorology classes certainly helped me understand the weather changes in Colorado. The Physical Geography classes have aided in understanding the various land formations found on the ranch. Bragging a bit, I did graduate with honors but I could not have done it without Art helping me study for the tests. He always says he furthered his education by going on the geography field trips when I had a class on Indiana geography. I should also mention that the professor for this class was from Minden, Nebraska and knew Art's brother there. It did not help on my grade as I worked twice as hard for this professor.

I received my degree in 1989 as Art was getting closer to an early retirement. He had been with Eli Lilly and Company for thirty-one years and it was time to plan for the future. The first question asked of me was, "where should we go to live?" We had talked about this before and had already decided we would not go to either Iowa or Nebraska. So now the immediate answer was "Colorado, of course." Colorado has sunshine for 360 days of the year. In Indiana, the clouds appeared early in October and stayed around for what seemed to be an eternity until about the first of May when activities at the Indianapolis 500 race track began. But with the sun came the humidity. In the summertime in Indiana, I could take a shower, dry off completely and still be soaking wet. So, of course, we would go back to Colorado. Also, for all of those thirty-one years, we had always found time and a way to get back to Colorado. Maybe not every year but at least every other one. That is, until we took up skiing. The ski areas in Indiana and even those in northern Ohio or southern Michigan were only hills, not mountains. We were spending every Christmas break in Colorado on the slopes and even spring breaks when possible.

A week or so later Art asked, "How about raising cattle?" The reasoning being we were still young. Just sitting around reading, playing bridge, or playing golf (even if it was only miniature golf) was not an option. So, my answer was, "Why not?"

A Plan In Motion

First and foremost was where in Colorado would we settle and how to decide? The location needed to be near an airport because we were leaving friends of 31 years as well as yet unborn grandchildren. Of course, when we left Colorado Springs, there were A LOT of open spaces so we were sure it would be easy to find land. Just how much was needed had not really entered our minds. Oops! How the area had grown. Now there were paved streets that had only been gravel before. Not to be discouraged, we started looking. Art had meetings in Denver so I tagged along and meeting up with local friends, we drove around looking for possibilities. When deciding on the general area, we met with a real estate agent and were on our way.

Now the question was "How much land are you interested in?" Well, we want to have a cow/calf operation. Next question, "What size herd will you be having?" Another OOPS! In Colorado, to maintain a cow and calf operation, it takes twenty acres per pair because of the lack of moisture. This information was vital to the decision of how many animals we wanted to have. We found a place in the right location with 800 acres which sounded about right for what we thought we wanted and it was OK, BUT! We went ahead and made an offer for the property and fortunately the owner decided not to sell. BOY! Were we lucky.

Another local real estate agent called us saying he had a place of 2,000 acres for sale but would divide it if we were interested. The question arose, "Will it take the same amount of buildings, etc. to raise cows/calves on 1,000 acres as it would have on 800?" "Yes. So back to Colorado we went. We met the agent, Clint Hoagland, who said we could have a look at the property but to do so we needed to hop in his trusty pickup truck (a new adventure for me). So off we went. Well, a pickup truck even one with four-wheel drive is not the most comfortable vehicle but to see the land, we had no choice. We were driven over at least 60 zillion bumps, down valleys, past yucca plants, over sage, around Ponderosa and Juniper pines and then to the most spectacular hill where the view was breathtaking.

The whole Front Range of the Rocky Mountains was spread out before us. The Spanish Peaks, located almost to the New Mexico border were to the south, Pikes Peak was to the near south, Mount Evans was due west and Longs Peak with its distinctive box like peak was to the north. Even beyond was what would be the mountains on the Wyoming border. What a panorama of beautiful mountains. But turning to the east, before us laid land of assorted color, with hills providing shadows for the valleys, cottonwood trees lining the banks of the creek, open blue skies, and a sky so blue it took our breath away.

Off in the distance we could see other ranch houses and even cattle roaming the hills. While still inspecting the property, a small herd of mule deer approached. They stopped, looked at us and said, "We will be happy to share this land with you." An offer was made and it was accepted so now Art and I were the proud owners of 1,000 acres with only a water tank and a windmill to supply the water for the future cattle.

One important part of this story was what the realtor did not tell us. South of what would become Eagles Nest Ranch was the unincorporated town of Elbert. Our first picnic on the ranch was on a large outcropping of rock looking across the road, down the creek valley eventually spotting the water tower by the school in Elbert. We tried to imagine what life was like as native Americans traversed this region. Later, doing research, it was discovered that Elbert and Elbert County have quite a history with many "firsts" being recorded.

The region of Elbert was "first" explored by John C. Fremont in 1843. The territory was established on February 28, 1861 with the "first" Territorial legislature meeting in Denver on September 9, 1861 thereby establishing 17 counties. Originally what would become Elbert County was part of Douglas County which stretched from the eastern side of the Rocky Mountains to the Kansas border. The "first" occupants were the Southern Cheyenne and Arapaho Indians. The "first" permanent settlers arrived in 1859. The "first" name of the town was Gomer's Gulch, because of Gomer's sawmill, located in the Kiowa Creek valley. It consisted of a post office, gambling halls and saloons. In reality, Gomer's Gulch was Gomer's ravine. The ravine filled up during torrential rain. Because of this natural phenomenon, the native Americans, who lived in the area, suggested that when plating the town of Elbert, it should be moved further downstream, away from the Kiowa Creek. Time will show that this advice was not totally heeded. Elbert, established in 1882 with the town plat filed on February 17, 1884, was named for Samuel H. Elbert. Mr. Elbert was described as an exceptional territorial governor and must have proven that to be true as was not only the town named after him, but so was the county and the main street through the town.

While there were settlements in the Elbert region prior to establishment of the actual town, the population increased greatly when the Denver and New Orleans

Built in 1906, The Russell Gates Merchantile Co. building is a must-see feature when passing through the town of Elbert.

Railroad was built through the area in 1881. Elbert became a thriving metropolis with three churches, a post office, hotels, a livery stable, a warehouse or creamery and a general store. The surrounding area was rural with the postman many times delivering baby chicks or milk/bread to the ranches/farms on his route. It was not long before the people of Denver, Colorado Springs, and Pueblo realized that Elbert with the elevation of 6,715 feet made it a perfect spot to spend the hot summer days in a cooler environment. Travel to Elbert was easily accomplished by riding the narrow gage railroad train which would stop in the middle of this town. As a result, today there are many small houses or cottages located within walking distance of where the train tracks had been. An actual train depot was built in 1891.

In the early 1900s there were many additional "firsts." An Elbert County Bank, one of two banks, was established. In 1901, Russell Gates built a private telephone line connecting his stores in surrounding towns. Following the established route of the Colorado and Southern Railroad the communication signal was transmitted through the barb wire fences and would eventually lead into his stores. One does question how such a line would be connected when having to cross a road, but not one resource covered this issue. In 1902, two grain elevators were added to the skyline. In 1906, a public school was put into operation as was the second or replacement of the Russell Gates Mercantile Store. The following years saw new telephone lines being built radiating out from Elbert. At this point a telephone exchange was established with the switchboard being located in a local hotel. Each subscriber had to furnish their own phone and making their own connection. There was a twenty-five-cent charge per month for services rendered. Whatever would these people think of today's services providing not only communication over the phone line but the possibility of sending photographs or extensive business documents, not only to immediate surrounding areas but worldwide.

Today the unincorporated town (meaning there is no local government—police services are supplied by the Colorado State Patrol) consists of two of the three original churches, a saloon which possibly was a general store, an auto repair shop and the Russell Gates Mercantile Building, now a community center cared for by the Elbert Women's Club. The post office still receives baby chicks but now the purchase must be picked up at the post office–no delivery. The Mini-mart serves as a "Pizza" shop, coffee stop for locals, a service station and a quick stop for items forgotten at the grocery store. There is a beautiful K-12 school built in 2016 with many students riding buses from the rural ranches and the many housing sub-divisions. A sports park is located in the flood plain where some of the original buildings were damaged in the 1935 flood. (See Conservation)

There is one distinct item remaining from the original railroad days. It is the foundation of the water tower for the train. It is a huge cement block adjacent to Elbert Road in the center of town. It probably goes unnoticed by most people passing through Elbert, but the longtime residents know for sure what it is and the part of history it plays. To learn more I suggest reading *Denver & New Orleans Railroad* by James R. Jones and *History of Elbert County* by Margee Gabehart.

Not Retirement, A New Vocation

Fast forward a year and a half. Retirement date was drawing near. What to do first! A barn was needed so Art began drawing plans similar to barns he had seen in Texas. It was decided that the barn needed a small apartment which would be used during the calving season. Second, what breed of cows would fill the bill? There are so many different breeds but each one is special for a specific reason, such as the altitude, weather conditions, calving ease, disposition and most important, which one would sell the best. After much research it was decided on commercial Black Angus cows to be crossed with Polled Hereford bulls. This combination would produce black, white-faced calves scientifically known as a F1 hybrid cross. My head was filled to capacity with all this important information. (I learned quickly that ranchers have a vocabulary all of their own.) The plan was to sell the F1 female (heifer) calves to other producers to be used as replacements in their herds. The male (steers) would go to feedlots to be fattened up and then slaughtered for meat. What a lot to learn!

Retirement date arrived and we loaded up what would be needed such as a workbench filled with important tools, a hide-a-bed for the weary ranchers, some cookware and other household necessities. Off to Colorado we went, leaving behind a home of twenty-seven years filled with furniture and memories that would be transferred to the new home when finished. A driveway had already been established, the barn and house were both under construction and electricity was available. The phone line was, sort of, operational but the only phone was up on the hill under a bucket with a huge rock on top. This was near where the house was being built but it was a quarter of a mile away from the barn straight up an elevation of two hundred feet. As we approached the gate to the ranch, we were welcomed with a sign and balloons placed by people who would become our near and dear neighbors. We were home but there was no house finished in which to live and there was a lot of work to be done before life on the ranch could be achieved. For the next three months we commuted from Denver where we were staying in a short-term apartment complex. During the day we would get started on all the work that was needed to become a working ranch.

First and foremost of importance was outfitting me in clothes appropriate for ranching. This meant buying jeans, a thing that had not been part of my closet since my teenage years—just a few more than a couple of years ago. Next a long sleeve shirt, not necessarily a new shirt, but one that would cover and thereby protect my arms when dealing with barb wire while building fences. Gone were the three-inch heels replaced with tennis shoes—not necessarily shoes with steel toes but ones with thick soles to protect my feet from cactus spines. But, of course, they would have to be washable in case the occupant, me, would accidentally step on a fresh cow patty. So much for fashion! A cowboy hat and fancy boots were purchased but only to be worn when flat landers came to visit or when we were selling cattle or going to the famous Western Stock Show in Denver.

Probably the smallest and most important item of clothing would be gloves. A pair of gloves does not necessarily mean "gloves." There are rubber gloves required when pulling calves when birthing. They are also needed when putting fly tags containing pesticide in the ears of cows and calves. These tags are used for controlling flies that attack the animals during the four or five summer months. If a person is driving through the country and sees a large group of animals huddled together in a corner of a pasture swishing their tails, they are trying to keep the flies off themselves as well as their close companions. There are cloth summer gloves that may be washed and used many times over when building or fixing a fence. They may also be used for picking up downed tree limbs, trash thrown over the fence by motorists or even picking up pine cones. This latter usage is done only when I have a craft project for party decorations or for dipping in paraffin to be used as fireplace starters.

Next are leather gloves, some with lining for additional warmth, or some to be used whenever a glove is needed. No matter how many gloves a rancher has, invariably there will not be a matching pair. Gloves are stuffed in pockets, under the truck seats, in tool boxes, left behind on projects or even dropped from the tractor somewhere in a field.

Gloves are a NECESSITY! —no matter what kind.

Sorting through gloves looking for a matched set to fit the next job.

NAMING THE RANCH

A rt and I were asked many times what our ranch was going to be called. Several discussions followed until one day a neighbor asked, "Did you know you have an eagle's nest on your land?" Wow! What a pleasant surprise. That, of course, would be the name and so it is. Eagles Nest Ranch of Elbert, Colorado.

Proud owners of the Eagles Nest Ranch. The adventure begins.

The eagle was a golden eagle with brown body feathers and a beautiful golden head. Its nest had been in the same huge tree since the mid 1930s and was repaired annually by the returning occupants. It was a great sight for the us to behold when the eagles produced their chicks in the spring. These babies were so ugly they were beautiful—white feathers and big black eyes. According to the book, *Birds of Colorado*, by Mary Taylor Gray, the fledgling period is 66 - 75 days. The hungry babies could be heard calling for food when the parents weren't fast enough. The nest itself was a three-foot-wide platform with a slight indentation in the center so it was fun to watch the young waddle across the nest. Even though the eagles deserted the nest a few years ago, it is still in the tree and is always an interesting stop when tours are given of the ranch. One beautiful story about the eagle was when Art's 96-year-old mother, Sarah, was visiting the ranch and she said she had never seen

Golden Eagles' nest, inspiration for the name of the ranch. Photo by Ty Newton

a golden eagle. It was a beautiful Colorado blue-sky day when the eagle was sitting on the very top branch of a Ponderosa Pine tree. With binoculars Sarah, who had macular degeneration, could clearly see the bird. All of a sudden, the eagle took off and started soaring, as if it knew there was an audience for which to perform. What a glorious sight and an experience none of the observers would never forget.

Not only did the ranch need a name, it also needed a brand. We found out that we are in a Brand Area which required one. The brand is permanently recorded along with the name and address of the owners. Art, being sort of an artist, drew up a brand that would look like the eagle's head but when recorded, it is 2 lazy J's and 2 slashes. To anyone with a terrific imagination it is a perfect eagles head. We had submitted a sketch of our purposed brand to the Colorado Brand Board and it was rejected. This meant we would have to think even harder now to come up with a different idea. Not so fast! We were at a cocktail party given by the National Cattlemen Association when the Brand Commissioner stopped by to visit with us. When I found out that he was the head man, I jokingly said, "How much money do I have to stick under the table to get our brand approved?" He laughingly asked what it had been, so Art described it. The Commissioner replied, "Why don't you add another slash making it "two lazy J's and two slashes. Resubmit it and I'll see what I can do." Was I ever embarrassed as I was just joking, not thinking he would take me seriously. We did what he suggested and it was approved. I guess maybe I spoke to the right person and I know I can never thank him enough. Now if this were still the wild west of years past, the brand could have stopped any cattle rustlers from stealing from this particular ranch. Today when hauling cattle and the truck goes through a weigh station, the driver, Art, will be asked for papers which give the identification of the cattle being hauled. If a rancher has had cattle stolen, this fact and identification of this cattle will be reported to the proper authorities. People at the weigh stations will be on the lookout for the cattle with the ranch brand and the culprit will be held. This hardly ever happens but it does provide a safety factor for the ranchers. One time I was driving the lead truck and pulled into the weigh station. This was my first time so when the Inspector, a Colorado State patrolman told me I had to come in, I did so but when he asked for the Brand registration papers, I was in a spot. I had to say, "I don't have them. They are in my husband's truck and he is about a mile behind me." Fortunately, he believed me so all was well and I went out, got in the truck and waited for Art.

Stopping at the Weigh Stations vary by state which I did not know. I was driv-

The Brand of Eagles Nest Ranch contains two lazy J's and two slashes, looking like the head of an eagle if you use your imagination.

ing, lead truck again, and not knowing I was supposed to stop in Nebraska, I just kept on driving, because if we are hauling our own cattle, we do not have to stop in Colorado. That lesson was learned after that time I stopped in Colorado. Of course, I should have known not to assume anything. RIGHT? This time, Art, being behind me, saw me go whizzing past so he was still laughing when he stopped and went in to be checked. He explained the situation and since he had the papers with him, no patrol person was sent after me. Just another lesson to learn.

Freeze Branding

Eagles Nest Ranch does "freeze branding" on our cows and calves. It is a procedure which involves a brass branding iron, an electric clipper, alcohol, dry ice and a timer.

The cows born on the ranch will be branded as calves. If replacement cows are purchased, they will be re-branded with the ranch brand, but this does not happen often since, for the most part, Eagles Nest Ranch produces our own replacements. The calves will be branded in June when they are about two months old by holding them down in a special squeeze chute in a position that exposes the left hip. The hair is shaved off in an area just large enough for a small brass iron. The space is sprayed with alcohol, the branding iron is removed from the cooler containing dry ice and alcohol, making the iron extremely cold, and then the iron is held on the calf's hip for fifty-five seconds, hence a timer is needed. This procedure does not damage the hide and is gentler on the animal than the hot branding iron. It takes over four or five weeks before the white hair appears because the hair follicles have lost the ability to pigment the hair. Needless to say, this procedure can only be used on dark haired animals.

There are still ranchers who use the method shown in western movies where they rope the calf, throw them on the ground and then take the branding iron from the nearby hot fire. The down side of hot branding is that it causes the hide of the animal to be devaluated by about twenty to thirty dollars as this part of the overall hide cannot be used for leather products.

Freeze branding does take a little longer as gathering supplies takes time and dry ice is not always easy to find, but this is done in conjunction with other procedures concerning the calves which is written about in other sections (See fly tags, shots, and castration). Of course, since we have never done the hot branding, we really can't say which procedure takes the longest.

The branding is being done by Art and helper, Trey, by holding the two month old calf down in a squeeze chute.

THE BARN, OUR WORKING HOME

Our barn is a "Pole Barn" described as a "farm building with no foundation supported by poles set in the ground typically at eight feet intervals." The poles in our barn are set at ten feet intervals with a lumber frame (40′ x 60′) covered with sheet metal over a concrete floor. The inside of the barn has six calving pens on the north side divided with steel swinging gates (another new term for me). In the middle of the barn, going lengthwise, is an alley made of gates fastened to steel posts with a connection allowing the gates to be swung in different positions or even removed, depending on the usage. This alley matches up with one coming in from the outside corrals. At the other end of the alley is a head catch made of two shaped steel pipes that may be pushed together for closure. It will be

The pole barn being constructed will be the center of life on the ranch.

released by using a hand lever. The cow's head will go between the pipes which will be closed around the cow's neck. This does not hurt the animal so it is not inhumane. It does take a lot of strength to pull the lever so the only one getting sore is the operator. The section of the alley holding the head-catch has as its floor an electronic scale covered by a wooden platform so that cows and calves may be weighed. This scale is also fun for visiting children as they step on it and their weight shows up on the electronic display hanging on the barn wall.

Showing pole construction and future positions of the pens marked out while building the barn.

Inside the finished barn showing the head-catch and individual pens.

On the south side of the building is our apartment which is used during the calving season from February thru the end of May, but in the beginning prior to building our home, it was our full time abode. Before this area was actually a functional living area, there was much work to be done by the two of us. Once the plumbing was operational, we would no longer have to commute to and from Denver so we moved our hide-a-bed into an empty space and began work on the interior. The barn builder, Danny Shaw, had left his chop saw (another new term) behind, making it available for us to use. Off we went with the red pickup to a lumber/hardware store in Denver to find the many needed materials. The apartment area already had the dry wall applied but we wanted more. Knotty pine paneling boards were found for the walls as well knotty pine lumber to be used for the cupboards and to cover the window frames. We searched for cupboards but the ready made ones were just too fancy to be placed in a barn. So once again, "Why Not?" We just made our own.

Inside the barn apartment, our home during calving season.

When the work actually began, the tools, lumber, safety glasses, gloves were all in order. When covering the walls with four-inch-wide pine boards, Art would get on the ladder and say, "I need a 45-degree left or right-angle panel board." Now I had never had a woodworking class in high school nor had I ever seen a "chop saw" which made frightening sounds when it was turned on, making me sure I would lose one or more fingers. I must admit it took me a while before I could get a board cut at the right angle. It took a great deal of thinking and holding my tongue just right before I made the cut. Before these boards could be positioned, they needed a wood sealer and then a stain, an easier job if done prior to hanging. Here is where the plastic gloves come in handy otherwise, my hand would have become slightly brown from the stain. A lot of turpentine on the hands helps though when the staining is finished. Putting the panels on the walls was not a real easy job. Supposedly, the panels could be placed on the walls with just a bit of glue on the back, but to be safe, we added some nails. Who wants the panels to fall off in the middle of the night?

After many days of work, the walls were finally covered, the next project was to make a table and benches as well as some other furniture out of #2 pine wood. Here again, we saw just what we wanted in a magazine but the size was all wrong. So, "Why Not?" We can do this! We used the previous design and made the table and benches as well as a frame for a futon out of #2 pine. To achieve the smooth but rustic appearance meant a lot of sanding, staining, and varnishing. Once again, it would not be correct to have fancy factory made furniture in a barn but, of course, very few people can say they "live in a barn." It was a lot of hard work but we were very pleased and proud of the results when the job was completed. To complete the project, I went to the fabric store and got foam and suitable fabric to make cushions so we did not have to sit on the hard benches.

All that time and work produced what would become the "great room" containing a small refrigerator, a micro-wave oven, a sink and a two-burner counter top stove. There is also a Futon, chairs, table, lamps, and of course, a TV. Down a hall is the bathroom with all the necessities, even pictures on the wall, and a bedroom, including a closet. The bedroom has a large window overlooking the corrals and during calving season I put a high Director's chair in front of what I call of my "window on the world" watching for cows in labor.

Back in the barn, next to the apartment is what is known as the "calf room." It includes a washer and dryer, a water heater, a freezer, a small refrigerator and cabinets holding all the calving necessities. Before the washer was there, I would go to the town of Elizabeth, fifteen miles away, to the laundromat to do the washing, then come home and hang the clothes over a line strung between three trees in the pasture up a hill from the barn. When the dryer was installed, no means of ventilation was provided which turned out to be a blessing in disguise. When a calf is born outside in inclement weather, it is brought into the "calf room," laid on a rug on the floor with the dryer hose directed at the calf's belly. The calf is covered with towels and the dryer heat is put on low allowing the calf to get warm and dry. This procedure is closely watched through the little window in the door. When the calf starts to move around and eventually stand up, we know the calf is warm and ready to be reunited with its mother who is standing by in one of the pens on the other side of the barn. How about that for dumb luck?

The last door opens to the supply room which is loaded with various important objects—too numerous to mention but very important to the daily operation.

When calving season is over and the branding and breeding is completed, this building is transformed into what might be called an "event center." The gates in the center alley and those in the individual pens are removed. The side gates of the pens are pushed to the back to the wall, thereby opening up the entire floor. Now the open space may be used for all types of events. The floor is scrubbed down with a pressure washer and treated with a bleach solution, making the area spotless.

My Window on the World

By now you have probably realized this is not an ordinary barn because it actually has windows. That is not to say other barns do not have windows because I am sure if there is an office in the barn, it will surely have at least one window. Our barn has four windows, not counting the two little ones in the doors and the one from the apartment looking into the pens. These windows are not what I would call "house" windows as they are medium size, sliding types and high enough from the floor that a high chair must be used in order to see out from a seated position. I put a Captains chair in front of my "window on the world" which is in the bedroom. The real purpose of this window is in the spring when we are calving, it is my job to watch for cows going into labor. On the window ledge is a pair of binoculars, a telephone for calling Art when he is needed to bring in a cow and my needlework when the cows in the corral are quiet. When one is suspect, she will be watched carefully for signs of labor, such as lying down, getting up, turning around and sniffing the ground. I must admit, I have had many cows perform these actions and have insisted she be brought in, only to release her hours later as her actions were a false alarm.

"Do you ever get lonely?" This question is often asked by visitors and my answer is "No, not really." You see, I have this "window on my world" that allows me to watch and be entertained by the calves in the west winter pasture. We had just had a bit of snow and what fun I had watching the calves run and jump in it, playing what I would call, "Fox and Goose." It is not unusual to see a young calf, who had been completely stretched out, napping in the shining sun, to wake up, look around to find someone to play tag with. There were two other calves, also sleeping soundly, when the first one went over to one, nudged him with his nose until this calf also was wide awake. Off they went, running as fast as they could with their tales sticking straight up in the air. Around the pasture they went but they both realized there was still a buddy asleep. Why not have a big game of tag, so off the two went, waking up the third calf. Of course, I could not hear "you're it" from any of these participants but the calves used their noses for tagging. It was easy to determine the calf who was it, as the other two took off in another direction. And so, it goes!

Another observation from my "window on the world" is in the spring when the mornings are cool, the cows will congregate in the corral about ten o'clock. They

My special window to the world, a place of constant entertainment when watching our cows.

will get their drinks of water and proceed to find their special spot where they will lay down. As the sun gets higher in the sky producing more heat, the dark, soft soil in the corral absorbs the warmth and the cows rest comfortably. The cows will stay there until about three in the afternoon where one by one they form a line, proceeding east around the dam to the winter pasture and grazing. All of these cows are pregnant so if I am closely watching them and I see one leaving the group by herself, I will call Art saying, "I think we've got one to bring in." A cow going off by herself is usually always a good indicator that she is getting ready to give birth. Now, since we can't see through the dam, the Gator or another vehicle is put to use. One of us will grab the ever-important binoculars and drive out to where the cow will be watched from a distance so as not to interfere with their giving birth. However, if bad weather is predicted, we watch her closely and will bring her either into the barn or preferably to the shed where she thinks she is in control and having her privacy. Little does she know we have a closed-circuit TV in the shed so are watching her every step of the way. Since our herd is small, we can do this where ranchers of large herds do not have this luxury.

I was looking out the window when I saw this cow walking back and forth at the fence line by the county road. She kept this up for quite a while so I assumed she had put her calf somewhere close by but could not find it. I went out to help her and found the little calf lying in a slight depression in front of the fence. The calf was sound asleep with walls of grass surrounding him and keeping him warm. She had been so close and yet so far away, as the saying goes. She knew that was where she had put her baby but nature was safely hiding the calf.

Many times, while watching the antics of the calves, I would call my friend, Nancy, and share with her what I was watching. She had also been a city girl and was always interested in my cow/calf observations from the "window on my world".

Eagles Nest Social Center

Serving as an event center, the barn has hosted birthday parties, Halloween parties, reunion gatherings and annual Church School picnics.

The birthday party began as a gathering of friends from Indiana who were in Denver for scientific meetings. At first it was to be for just a few people (13) and normally it would have been held at the house but as the word got out, more and more people (45) were going to be coming. This was in August and monsoon time of the year meaning there could be a lot of muddy feet. Being rather selfish, I really did not want 45 individuals in the house so quickly plans were made to move this celebration to the barn. I quickly borrowed tables and chairs from the local church and since it was summer, the barn was already spotlessly clean. The grill was set up outside where steaks were prepared and everyone brought food to share. One of the families' daughters was celebrating her birthday so her cake was to be served as the dessert. Problem was that the cake was accidently dropped on the floor but the thirty second rule went into effect. The cake was carefully attended to, some of the frosting was rearranged making the cake eatable and enjoyed by all.

A Halloween party was held for the children of parents in the Biology Department from the Air Force Academy. It was decorated with streamers hanging from the rafters and ghosts made from sheets supposedly flying through the air. The children, even with some performing tricks, were given small buckets and went from table to table getting treats handed out by the parents. There was a tub filled with water where the youngsters were to rescue an apple but this was not utilized as the participants, from babies to some adults, were dressed in costumes and really did not want to get wet. A great time was had by all and is still remembered by the members of the Biology Department.

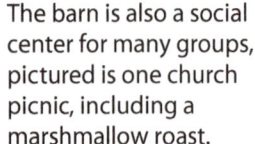

The barn is also a social center for many groups, pictured is one church picnic, including a marshmallow roast.

Plenty of food and fun times are had by all. Friends make the ranch a home.

The Church School picnic began as a small gathering of about 80 people but as the years passed, the crowd grew to more than 130. This is not an ordinary picnic, as not only is great food supplied so too is entertainment. The visitors are always treated to a hay ride tour of the ranch. While on the hay ride, the visitors ask questions and are told stories about activities on the ranch. They are most interested in how and why we came to Colorado and how we got into the ranching business. After one such time, one of the ladies insisted that I should write a book as our experiences and adventures needed to be told. Every year the same people go on the hay rides, hear the same stories and maybe some new ones depending on what may have happened of interest during the past year. This book is a result of her insistence and encouragement.

Identifying wild flowers for table decor was much more enjoyable than collecting cow patties, but not as funny.

No one picnic is like another. One time the visitors had to identify the wild flowers found in the fields. When all collected, the flowers made terrific table decorations. Another time a cow-patty toss was part of the entertainment. To accomplish this, two city women, Carol Comes and Janis Seifert were sent out to the pasture to collect dry patties. It is hard to describe their reaction when they were told what they were to do but they relented and were successful. I was very kind and gave them gloves so they wouldn't get their "city" hands dirty. Of course, their first reaction was, "You want us to do what?" Lots of laughs were had by all.

Probably the funniest time was when the entertainment was sort of a talent show. It was being held on the outside of the barn with the audience sitting on blankets on the hill. All of a sudden, I looked to the southwest of the barn and saw this huge black cloud. In Colorado when there is a black cloud anywhere close by, you do not wait to see which way it is moving. Everyone picked up their blankets and moved into the barn. The show must go on! It did, but the black cloud positioned itself over the barn, dropping huge raindrops and hail on the metal roof. It got so loud, the beautiful music being sung by a women's quartet was completely drowned out.

One other time, people were told not to bring desserts as a marshmallow roast had been planned. A pit fire was all ready and participants had sticks loaded. Graham crackers and Hershey bars were ready to go but all of a sudden, there was a loud clap of thunder. Once again, action is taken quickly. Everyone turned and ran to their cars and to this day, we do not know where the crackers, marshmallows, chocolate bars and sticks ended up. Everyone took something but it is doubtful that a "s'more" was ever successfully made. It remains one of the most talked about picnics ever of the 16 that have been held to date.

After those two experiences, changes were made. A proper stage was obtained from the church and placed in the west end of the barn. Individual chairs were brought by the audience and arranged in front of the stage. The entertainment became more involved. Now, there were melodramas that required audience participation—that of cheering or booing at the appropriate time. There were take-offs on television game shows such as "What's My Line" or "I've Got A Secret." There was even a spectacular show with a vocalist doing Elvis songs. The stage back is the barn doors covered with four panels decorated/painted to go along with the theme of the show. As with all church functions where food is served, the picnics were no exception as everyone brought their favorite recipe and a huge appetite. No one ever left hungry and this day was always special for the attendees.

The picnic was usually the last bit of annual entertaining in the barn so with help from many volunteers, the gates are all replaced, the feed tubs returned to the stalls, the individual water units turned on and the barn is ready for use.

The next time the barn will be used is when preparations are made for the cows being moved to Nebraska for winter camp. (This is covered later) When the cows are gone, the barn is once again thoroughly cleaned, supplies are inventoried and needs recorded. Preparations are made for the next years activities.

The finished barn and social center for Eagles Nest Ranch with one of our first improvements, the shed.

Improvements and Additions

Shed

One of the most important additions to the facilities was the building of a shed. It is built similar to a barn, but it has only three walls. The two ends are closed with overhead doors while the long back wall is covered with metal barn siding. Inside the shed are six stalls or pens divided by gates able to move either right or left, to adapt to needs at the time. Some cows do not like to give birth in an enclosed area (barn) as it does not seem to be their nature. With the shed clearly open on the remaining long side, the cows think they are less confined in a more natural situation.

Unfortunately, there are no individual water tanks in the pens so tubs are used both for feed and water. The water is obtained from hoses connected to outside hydrants. Electricity in the shed allows for submergible water heaters to be used during the winter, keeping the water thawed.

There are gates across the open side of the shed which lead to three corrals. One corral is used as a shelter for the whole herd when "first alert" weather is eminent. The end pen has a gate with the bottom two bars free to open separately from the top so when there is snow, the calves can get under the gate into the pen out of the snow. There is straw spread out in the pen. The mothers are left outside but close enough for the calves to go out when they get hungry. In a sense, the shed also serves as a snow shelter as the closed back side faces the north and prevailing winds.

There was one night when we woke up to a terrible snow storm. The snow was blowing horizontally and there were cows and small calves in the corral. The end doors had been installed only the day before, so this was certainly a "let's see how this all works" time. We got dressed so quickly, we didn't bother to put on our "weather gear." It did take a while to get the cows and calves separated but the system worked just fine. Needless to say, it was a very short night for sleeping. The only problem was that it took three days for our coats to dry because it was a terribly wet snow.

Flood Lights

The first year of calving for us began in early February. In Colorado there is always the chance of snow in February through even early May. The cows that year were first time heifers, meaning this was their first calf and prone to having problems. We, also lacking prior experience, were overly cautious, so every day when feeding, heifers looking most promising would be moved from the pasture into a corral closest to the barn. When the day light, providing easy observation turned to the darkness of night, a new plan of attack was implemented. We would take turns during the night watch which meant setting the alarm clock to go off every three hours. When the alarm went off, the one having night duty would get up, get completely dressed in coveralls, boots, heavy coat, stocking cap, with some differences depending on the weather. On the way out the door, a flashlight would be grabbed. As time went on, the flashlight would be replaced by a lantern with higher power. The unlucky person doing the night duty would go to the corral and working their way through the herd, check each animal to see if any needed to be taken into the barn to give birth.

This procedure went on for a few years when the most important improvement was accomplished. LIGHTS! Flood lights were installed. They could be activated with a flip of a switch inside the barn and VOILA! The whole corral with its occupants could be seen. This was not an overnight project as two poles had to be strategically spaced, the power line had to be buried and light fixtures installed. The lighting of the corral proved to be marginal so in later years more flood lights were added to both poles. With time, more improvements were made, especially replacing the old lights with brighter and more efficient LED lights.

The lights did not mean we could give up their every three-hour checking. Now we can just get out of bed, go to the "window on the world," grab the binoculars, get the sleep out of our eyes, and hopefully focus so as to not to miss an animal possibly in labor. Of course, if there is activity in the corral, the old procedure of getting fully dressed would be accomplished in a hurry.

Closed Circuit Television

After the modern invention of lighting for the corral, came the ultimate improvement. The installation of a closed-circuit television system in the shed. It has three cameras that focus on the six calving pens and one camera focusing on the barn corrals. The cameras have night vision, making the night viewing as clear as the day views. Each camera can be focused on an individual area and cows of interest. The system is connected to a television set in the bedroom of the barn. The TV will be left on all night and checked when the phone alarm goes off every two hours. So now all we have to do is just raise our head off the pillow, check the monitor and if nothing is happening, go back to sleep. How easy is that—we don't even have to go to the window and possibly fall over the chair. Of course, if we are fully awake the television image may quickly be switched from watching the expectant cows, in not only the shed but also the corral to a Hallmark movie! Isn't modernization wonderful?

Solar Power

Another improvement was the installation of solar power to replace the aging windmill. The windmill, quite possibly had been installed in the 1920s but was still operational when we bought the land. It was replaced in the barn corrals by an electric pump and eight automatic electric water tanks which keeps water flowing during the winter months. The windmill was moved and a new water tank was installed in the center of the summer grazing pastures. When the windmill reached the point of no repair in 2019, it was replaced by two 3 x 3-foot solar panels which control the electric DC pump in the 260 foot deep well. When it is cloudy, the pump may produce just a trickle of water but when the clouds move past and the sun appears, the pump will produce five to seven gallon per minute. According to the Colorado Tourist Information, the sun shines 360 days a year so presumably, the ranch will never run out of water. During the summer months, when the tank and overflow tank are both filled, the pump may be turned off manually. During the summer, a mature cow may drink twenty-five gallons of water per day.

The windmill is one of the most photographed objects on the ranch and even though nonfunctional, is a great talking point. It was originally made by Dempster Mill Manufacturing Company in Beatrice, Nebraska. Charles Brackett Dempster, known as CB Dempster purchased an interest in a small windmill and pump shop where his job was to erect the windmills and install pumps. In 1885 he began manufacturing his own windmills, with the first model being known as the Original Dempster Solid Wheel. He created five models of these solid-wheel mills with the first being the Queen City, produced in 1892. By 1922, Dempster was selling self-oiling windmills which were manufactured for over eighty years with minimal modifications. The mill on Eagles Nest Ranch was a "Dempster No. 12 Annu-Oiled (Babbitt & Hyatt roller bearings). It was the company's first self-oiling back-geared windmill, meaning oil was needed only about once a year. This particular windmill model is said to be the most frequently seen in almost all areas of the United States as well as in many foreign countries.

Both the automatic electric water tanks in the barn corrals and the solar well system have proven to be 100% better than the original systems, especially in the winter when the water in the large tank would be frozen and we would have to take shovels, pitchforks and sledge hammers out to daily break the ice. Neither of us never tried to break the ice by just standing on it, which, of course, would NOT be a good idea!

The windmill, next to a solar panel, is one of
the most photographed items on the ranch.

PLEASE FENCE ME IN!

The barn was well under construction when we arrived to be permanent residents of Elbert, Colorado but it was not ready for occupancy. There was work to be done! We had a choice. We could hire someone to build the fence while we sat in lawn chairs watching or we could dig in and do it ourselves. "Why Not! I know WE can do it!"

When we bought the land there was a perimeter fence around the whole property but since we had bought only the south end and since this is not "open range" country as seen in western movies, a fence defining the new property line was necessary. A professional fence builder was hired to build this mile and one-half section. It was one of perfection so we realized we had quite a job ahead of us. Farmers and ranchers have a reputation to live up to by presenting straight lines of fences to people passing by and we certainly did not want people to think that since I was a city girl, I wouldn't know how to build a proper straight-lined fence.

The first project for us was to divide the south end of the ranch into what would become the winter pasture. This would be an interior fence so it was a perfect place to learn on how to make a "professional looking" fence. But to do so required one vital piece of equipment. A Truck! How else could we get all the materials needed? A pickup truck with four-wheel drive was definitely a must. Our currently owned sedans just would not work so when browsing the local newspaper, a used truck dealer was found. There on the lot was a red 1988 Ford 250. Perfect! It wasn't a fancy truck but it did have a working radio and a bed large enough to hold all the required posts and barbed wire. This red truck will be a subject throughout the rest of the story so be prepared for lots of laughs.

All of a sudden Art and I both realized our wardrobe of years past would not and could not be used for ranching. Since we still had our house in Indiana, we had left most of our clothes behind. Art had been wearing a suit and tie to work for thirty-one years. I had made most of my clothes and this didn't include jeans. I could not be building fences in Pendleton wool slacks or fancy one piece jump suits, fashionable at the time. Art had been involved with the Boy Scout troop so he had plenty of jeans and shirts suitable for ranching. He just looked at me and said, "We've got to go shopping!" Jeans, T shirts, tennis shoes, boots, and long sleeve shirts were needed. The shirts I could salvage from Tim and Greg's closets as they had outgrown them. But for me, the Kohl's bags kept filling up and getting heavier and heavier. One time though, I was lucky and found a feminine blue work shirt with ruffles on the front—which would be saved for a non-working but a "ranch experience day" such as going to a stock show. All I needed now were gloves! No more long white ones to be worn with formals, no more short black, brown or white ones to be worn with a suit or winter coat. These gloves had to be leather or heavy cloth material; color was not important. Serviceability was first and foremost. When the gloves were purchased, we were ready for work. Let the fence building begin.

The tools in the Indiana workbench were immediately put to use as the building was begun. Here again, it was not to be just any fence as we would discover. This fence would serve as the boundary line for the winter pasture. It would run for one mile from the east side of the ranch to the west with two corrals in the center section with the barn located on the north. The barb wires were to be six inches off the ground so the pronghorns could slither under. The top wire was to be no higher than 48 inches so the deer could jump over. These rules were so noted.

The first step in building a fence is to set wood stakes to mark the location for the fence posts. It is important to the ego of the ranchers that the fence be perfectly straight. Many times, this meant I was on my stomach lining up the stakes giving signs with my hands, waving a little more to the right or to the left and then crossing the arms to say OK, thereby aligning the original stake that had been placed many yards away. Of course, a professional fence builder would have had a transit making the job much easier. A stake was pounded into the ground at the far end and a string laid on the ground between the two stakes thereby creating a straight line. Next came the measuring part with a long measuring tape and a can of spray paint to mark the location of each post.

An eight foot by eight-inch diameter wood anchor post was positioned at the beginning and end of the fence line, each quarter mile or any place where the line of sight is disturbed either by a hill or a change of direction. On one side of the anchor post is a similar one spaced eight feet away with a wire brace strung from the top of one post to the bottom of the other. This configuration keeps the posts upright preventing them from being pulled in the direction of the stretched wire. In the fence line wood posts will be positioned at forty-eight or sixty-foot intervals, depending on whether the fence is a perimeter fence or an interior one. In between the wood posts will be three evenly spaced steel posts. Marking completed! Let the digging begin!

One of the many steps in fencing the ranch, with a tractor-mounted post hole digger. Let the digging begin!

The digging involved using a tractor equipped with a post hole digger doing the work. Here's where our good neighbors, Al Colyer and Dan Audrey, came to the rescue. Not only did they know what to do, they also had the equipment. The post hole digger is an auger (looks like a large cork screw) mounted on the back of a tractor and moves up and down by a hydraulic lift. A three-foot-deep hole was dug. A yardstick is put in the hole, making sure the hole is three foot deep. If not, a strong man would have to take a post hole digger, with two cup like pinchers mounted on two four-foot wood handles and go down into the hole, dig out the dirt, bringing it to the surface, one pinch at a time until the necessary three feet measurement was achieved. Then an eight feet pole five to six inches in diameter is put in it. It was my job to use the level making sure the pole is straight from all directions. Next, I got to pour the dry cement into the hole. As water is added, Art, with a long pole, mixed the two together around the pole so it will be solidly secure. The dirt that had been pulled out is now placed back in the hole and is pounded down with a steel tamping rod with an enlarged circular bottom about three and a half inches in diameter. The final step is to place any extra dirt around the post. Our land had been rented out previously to a neighbor for cattle grazing so we had to not only watch where we walked but had to make sure they had clean soil around the posts. I accidentally put and old cow patty in the hole but quickly had to dig it out and replace it with good dirt because dry cow patties do not pack!!!!

The second step is to place steel "T" posts at measured intervals between the wood posts. These posts have steel tabs protruding out at inch intervals on one side. Placing these posts is a terribly hard job but is made easier when a STRONG young man is doing the pounding. There is a special tool called a "fence post pounder," which is a two feet long cylinder with weight at the top closed end and handles on either side. It fits over the steel posts so with every downward motion the post is driven into the ground.

When clipping wires to the posts, the "clippee" must constantly be on the lookout for Prickly Pair cactus when kneeling! The needles are quite difficult to remove.

The third step involves stringing of the barb wire. Dan was the expert of this job and my job was to measure and mark on the wood posts where the wires were to be placed. Here again rules are to be followed. If the fence is an exterior one, it will require five stands of wire thereby making the fence so strong a cow would not be able to get out. Interior fences only need four. The barb wire is always strung on the inside of the wood and T posts giving the fence added strength.

All at once there were new terms to be used. "Clip and staple." Now in my language a clip was a thing to hold papers together or to hold hair in place. A staple was a little wire that with the aid of a stapler, papers would be securely fastened together. Fencing clips and staples will hold the wire to the posts but they are definitely different not only in shape but in size. The clips are a funny shaped piece of wire, about the diameter of a clothes hanger that is wrapped around the steel post and over the barb wire of the fence so as to keep the wire securely in place. The staples are horseshoe shaped nails with barbs (another new word) on the side and are pounded over the barb wire into the wood posts, once again fixing the wire securely in place.

Back and forth the hard-working red pickup went spreading out the barb wire. When it was in place, out came the hammers, staples, wire stretchers, wire cutters, and of course, gloves and safety glasses. Starting six inches from the ground, the first length of barb wire is wrapped around the anchor post and secured tightly with staples. The wire is laid on the ground between the first anchor post and the one at the end of the quarter mile section. Here the wire will be pulled tight between the posts with a tool known as a "wire stretcher." When tightened to the desired amount, the wire will be wrapped around the post and stapled securely in place. This continues until all wires are correctly spaced and are either stapled or clipped in place. Please note that when clipping barb wire to the T posts, one must be careful not to tighten the wire too much as the wire will break and splicing the wire back together is not an easy job nor does it make the foreman happy! I was doing my job of clipping the wire to the T post and I apparently didn't know my own strength because the wire just snapped. Dan came to my rescue and politely said, "You do not need to clip quite that hard!" He was laughing all the time. He was extremely kind!!!

Many miles were walked during the fence building operations but what a glorious sight when they were finished and the fence was in a perfectly straight line. Building a fence is exhausting work but it is also very rewarding when the posts are all straight and the wires are not drooping. It is also a time well spent with nature as some of the smaller birds fly from post to post hoping to find bugs to eat while the Meadowlark provide music for the workers.

When this first operation was completed, I wrote back to Dean Barbara Jackson at IUPUI that I really hadn't needed my college degree to work on building fences. I had already learned how to count to ten when I was three years old and now, I really only had to count to six. She appreciated my sense of humor.

Corral Fences

Once the line fences were in place, work on the corral fences began. Here the wooden posts were spaced eight feet apart with long lengths of heavy hog wire panels being stapled to the posts. Then 2" x 6" x 16 feet lengths of treated wood were positioned at the top and centers of the wire. When completed, the area would serve as a permanent corral, large enough for many pregnant cows at one time. The corral being close to the barn enabled both of us to carefully watch the cows for any birthing activity. The second corral to the west was built in the same manner and in between both is the original water tank. The fence between the two corrals has a gate providing an opening when separating cows for various purposes. Here again I had to learn the difference between a gate and a panel. Basically, they look alike except gates are permanent fixtures and are made to swing in either direction where a panel is stationary and used in making temporary corrals.

Gates

Gates are used on Eagles Nest Ranch for entrances into daily and frequently opened pastures and/or corrals. They are connected to a wooden fence post with latches to be opened and closed by humans. However, there was one time when we forgot to check if the gate was securely fastened which leads to another story.

We were sitting in the barn apartment and could see branches of the nearby trees moving. "What is going on. I don't see the tree branches in the pasture moving" I said. Upon looking out the window we saw these black objects pulling down low branches, thereby making all branches move. "Oh, my gosh" was my response. "The cows got out of the pasture." What happened next was a "round up" and a pushing back of the cows who knew exactly where they were supposed to go. My only comment was "I guess the grass was greener on this side of the fence!" All cows were counted and none had gone further away so that adventure ended well. Instead of a sign reading, "Turn off the lights when leaving," we need a sign saying, "Be sure the gate is securely closed when leaving." Cows cannot resist an open gate!

As we got older and much wiser, we placed "people gates" at various locations so we could get into the corrals at the barn without having to walk the fence line to the nearest open cattle gate. This also meant no more having to climb over the fence and certainly much safer.

Wire Gates

There are also wire gates which are the same configuration of the wire fences in the pastures. They are hooked to the wood post by hoops of wire, one at the top of the gate post which loops over the wood post at the end of a fence line. There is a loop on the bottom of that post which allows the gate post to sit securely at the bottom while also being secure at the top. This works fine except when I try to open or close the gate. The men in my family say simply, "Put your shoulder into the gate post and the wire will lift off very easily." That is all fine except they are all taller than me. To fix this dilemma, the men put a device called a "cheater" on the line post that is steel with a loop that fits over the gate post. There is also a handle that pulls the whole operation together and "Voila" the gate is closed!

Panels

If gates and panels are stored together, from a distance they are hard to differentiate. Panels are used when a temporary corral or working area is needed. They come is a variety of lengths from six feet to sixteen feet and are so heavy it takes two people to position them. When moving panels from the storage stack to the working area, the tractor with the grapple hooks do the work.

The panels have two narrow vertical tubes (about the size of a women's thumb) strategically spaced on one end side. On the other side are two open holders which fit over the tubes when the panels are connected. When all the panels are correctly positioned for the task at hand, the first and last panels will be securely wired to existing permanently placed wood fence posts.

This type of configuration provides a smaller corral for the new born calves and mothers as the await the arrival of other pairs. When there are five or six pairs, they will be released to the larger pasture where there will be safety in numbers against any predators.

Electric Fencing

Strands of electric fencing are used in an area around the house so the cows and calves will not eat the nice grassy area known as the front lawn. In this case, power for the fences is provided through a long extension cord from the house. Electric fencing is also used in more remote areas where temporary fences are needed. Here solar panels or car batteries are used in providing the electricity. This, unfortunately, does not always work to perfection.

One day, I looked out the front window of the house, only to see a heifer just chomping away on the beautiful grassy lawn. I went out and said, "What do you think you are doing?" The heifer raised her head, wiggled her ears, looked at me and continued to eat. She finally stopped eating, turned, slowly walking over to the electric fence, jumped as if it wasn't even there, and continued out to the pasture. Everything was fine until the next day when the very same heifer was back again enjoying the nice green grass that she hadn't eaten the day before. This time, the heifer knew she had better leave, which she did. The electric wire was now raised making it harder for her to jump. This type of fencing gives, the animal or person, a slight shock but it is never harmful to either when contact is made. One interesting point it that when an animal comes in contact with the fence, they remember what the wire is and what the outcome might be so they instinctively stay away from it even when it is not charged.

Repairing an Existing Fence

Each spring before turning the cows and calves out to the large pasture, every line of wire in the fences is checked. A properly constructed fence will last for many years. On the Eagles Nest Ranch there is one section of fence which could possibly have been there since the 1920s. We were told by a local rancher that this land had once been used for raising horses so the top two wires of the fence were made of smooth wire. Narrow tree trunks were used with the wires being tied to the posts. Some of the trunks were straight and others, not so much. As a result, fixing this stretch is truly a challenge.

Since quite often it was my job to don my carpenter's apron, with pockets filled with a hammer, staples and clips, I would drive the golf cart along the fence line looking for loose wires. When one would be spotted, I would with hammer in hand, either re-pound the old staple in the wooded post or replace the old one with a new one. Other times the wires had been stretched, pulling the clips off the T posts. Here again, with my special tool used for clipping, the wire would be clipped to the post and off I would go to the next one. These problems are easily fixed but when the wire has been broken or drastically stretched, I would need Art's strong arm. To remember where the break was, I would tie an orange plastic ribbon near the break and when time permitted, both of us would work together fixing the problem.

(Please note the addition of a golf cart to the fencing operation. Since we were close to retirement age, it was decided there would be no horses on this ranch and only mobile vehicles would be used. Plus, the fact that horses would eat the grass needed for the cows and calves).

Unfortunately, the challenge of fixing an existing fence was given to me before I actually became a rancher. I had come from Indiana to spend a day with Greg fixing part of the exterior fence already in position on the ranch. It was a cold day in May and the neighbors would be renting the pasture until Eagles Nest was established. What a sight I was. My boots were too big and heavy. The gloves were too large as they were for men. My coat was bulky and the long sleeves made hand work difficult. Greg had given me a pair of long nose pliers so I could wind the clip around the barb wire and to the steel post. Problem was, the fingertips of the gloves kept getting in the way of the pliers. This made progress extremely slow and very frustrating. The next job was to pound the staples into the existing wood posts. Since this wood was very old and very hard, I thought for sure the wood was petrified. To make matters worse, off to the southwest the clouds were lowering and thickening, meaning a storm was eminent.

Artist, Jerry Palen from Wyoming drew this sketch of Flo's experience fencing. It states: "When you finish with your ranch, you can come to my place and help."

The temperature was dropping and by the time the last staple was in, it was snowing. How about that for an introduction to ranching. Shortly after that experience of fixing fence, I had the most wonderful opportunity of meeting Jerry Palen, a cowboy artist from Wyoming. He asked me what I had been doing lately and after I said, "Nothing" Art said, "You have been busy fixing a fence at the ranch." As we stood there conversing, Mr. Palen drew me a picture of his trademark, FLO. Flo's boots are oversized, as were her gloves. She has a scarf on her head, barb wire strung out beside her and cows looking over her shoulder. This drawing hangs proudly on my kitchen wall and I smile every time I pass it. That definitely was me. The only thing missing that first time were the cows looking over my shoulder. That came later and is exactly how the cows react. They are so nosey and must check out our every operation.

Since I had said "Why Not?" when asked about ranching, I could not be a quitter. I never had second thoughts about my future as a rancher. But one thing for sure, those old wood posts would have to be replaced.

Repairing a modern-day fence is not an everyday job but is a necessity when a car goes off the road and through the fence possibly breaking all wires. The wires of the fences may also be broken as a result of heavy snow drifts causing the wires to stretch. Cows leaning over the fence to get to the grass (which is always greener) on the other side also causes stretching. Top wires may be broken as the deer jump over or the bottom wires may break as the pronghorns slide under. Either way, the wires need to be fixed. For this, I decided it was like using a recipe so I put together a list. This way no one would have to drive back to the barn for a most important piece of equipment.

My check list:
1. Container to hold all small items
2. Wire, barb and smooth on roll
3. Wire stretchers - too large to put in container but place next to box
4. Wire cutter
5. Hammers
6. Staples
7. Clips
8. Fencing tools: long nose pliers and special clipping tool for me
9. Splicers
10. Crimpers to secure the splicers
11. Safety glasses
12. GLOVES!

If the wire has been stretched, it is cut and one end threaded into the "wire stretcher." The broken ends are each put into a cylinder, called a splicer, about 5/8 inches long and wide enough to hold two wires side by side. The fence wire is tightened and when satisfactory, the splicer is crimped securing the wires in place. The wire is then either stapled to the posts or clipped to the T posts. If the wire is completely broken, a piece of wire is cut from a big roll of barb wire and set aside. Both ends of the broken wire will be made into a loop. The previous mentioned piece of wire will be put through one loop and the wire will be twisted, also making a loop. The wire will be threaded in the wire stretcher and the straight piece of wire will be put through the loop on the other end. The wires will be stretched to the desired tightness and the straight piece of wire will be tightly wrapped around itself, closing all loops. Please note that this project, with all the newly acquired tools with strange sounding names was again a "first" for me, so many times Art was handed the wrong instrument. One might think that repairing fences would be a rather dull experience. While it is routine, why it needs repairing always leads to interesting stories.

One day as Art was driving the truck and I was riding/walking the fence line, I got out of the truck to tighten a clip. I stepped down to the ground and at that instant a baby pronghorn jumped up. I let out a yelp and the pronghorn ran off but not before making a hissing sound. It is yet to be decided which one was the most surprised. The fence was repaired. I got back in the truck and the baby pronghorn went back to the spot where his mother had told him to stay.

A major fence repair was needed when a spring downpour washed out three lines of fencing. It was not the rain that did the damage, it was caused by debris from upstream. The neighbor had piled wood in an area of a natural water runoff so everything was washed downstream as the water flowed toward the creek.

The water ran through the closest neighbor's ground tearing down the property line fence. It continued at a very high rate through the culvert onto the dry creek bed on the Eagles Nest Ranch bringing with it the wood and weeds found along the way. The water reached the check dam where the rate of flow was slowed but when that section of pasture dried out, three fences had to be replaced and debris removed. (See conservation chapter).

Another experience was when we had already gone to bed but were not asleep. I had turned over in bed, facing the window, when I saw lights on the trees. "Did you see those lights?" I asked Art. "No," he replied. At about the same time there was a loud knock at the back door of the house. The house is about 3/4 mile from the main road so who would be coming at this time of night? Art grabbed his robe and headed for the door. I did the same but I also grabbed the phone in case the sheriff was needed. No need to call as it was the sheriff standing at the door. He asked, "Do you have cattle in the pasture down by the road?" A driver of a pickup truck pulling an empty dog trailer had lost control of the trailer and it had gone airborne over the fence landing about 20 feet into the pasture. Fortunately, there were no cattle there so the trailer could wait until morning to be removed but dog food was found scattered throughout the grass.

Another non-life-threatening experience involved a handicapped man who said he was reaching for something on the floor of his car thereby losing control of the vehicle. He wiped out seven posts in a row which were sixteen feet apart leaving a huge gap. He was not hurt and immediately notified the ranchers, adding that he was willing to pay for repairs but he could not physically help with the work. He left saying he would be right back and when he returned, he had brought the minister from the local Christian Church who had been raised on a farm in Nebraska and knew exactly how to fix a fence. This fence repair resulted in a new friendship as the pastor and Art realized they knew some of the same people in Nebraska.

In one winter, people went through various parts of the fence seven times. Many repaired it themselves with whatever wire they had. It was not up to Eagles Nest standards so the repairs had to be replaced. Just another day in the lives of ranchers!

The Faithful old Red Truck

The ever-faithful 1988 red stick shift Ford F250 pickup was replaced by a new white 2005 Ford 350 pickup, although you will still read more about the red truck throughout this book. The new truck was still a stick shift but this one had a flatbed

Grandson Michael learned to drive in the old red truck. With the aid of a pillow behind him, he was able to reach the pedals.

which made hooking up the cattle trailer much easier. In the middle of the flat bed is a square hole with a round ball that is connected to the arm reaching out from the trailer. When connected, the truck driver has control over the lights and brakes of the trailer. The red truck remained part of the ranch long enough for both grandchildren to learn how to drive a stick shift while having one foot on the clutch and the other on the accelerator as they downshifted in order to make it up the steep hill on the ranch driveway. This was a lesson not taught in Drivers Education classes but considered important to learn. Eventually this truck was hauled off the ranch on a flatbed truck by a young man who planned on reconditioning it. We aren't really sure what happened to the "good ole' red pickup" but heard it was up and running once again. After a period of time, could it possibly be put in a museum as the "longest running, hardest working truck" ever to be sold?

The hard-working old red Ford truck, such a part of the ranch, shown here with the new truck behind..

WHEN IS A COW NOT JUST A COW?

As every young child is taught, a cow is an animal either pictured in a book about farm animals or is a four-legged animal standing behind a fence, eating the green grass in the pasture. Whichever the situation, the child is always told this creature is a cow that says "Moo." The youngster is taught to say "Moo" whenever they are asked what does the cow say?

As a child raised on a farm grows into adulthood, the definition of a cow changes, not drastically but more information is added. Such as, a male cow can either be classified as a "Bull" or a "Steer" depending on the situation. The female cow will be a "Heifer," then after her first calf she will be known as a "First Calf Heifer." Finally, after two and one-half years and has reached maturity, she will be a "Cow." For me as a city girl, this information had never been part of my education and now was an important lesson for me. Just something more to learn!

There are many different breeds of cows. Some are bred strictly to produce milk and "No, chocolate milk does not come from brown cows!" Others, such as the Brahmas are raised in areas primarily in the southern United States with tropical temperatures because they are able to tolerate the humidity and high temperatures. There are breeds of cows raised for the soul purpose of producing meat for human consumption and then there are cows and bulls raised strictly for production of mother cows.

We had decided the purpose of the cows and bulls raised on the Eagles Nest Ranch would be to produce "Cross-bred" heifers or those classified as "F1" s meaning the cow will be mated with a male (Bull) cow of a different breed. The bulls, preferably will have a reputation and statistics for growth and gentleness. The F1 heifers will be sold as replacement cows in commercial herds. We knew what our goal was but now the job was to find the correct combination of breeds.

We had purchased the ranch in 1990 but Art would not be retiring until 1992 so we had two years to find the perfect combination. Here again, I had so much to learn. We attended the National Cattlemen Association meeting in San Diego where Art was representing Eli Lilly and Company. While he was in scientific meetings, I joined the other wives in a "classroom discussion" concerning all sorts of matters. I was faithfully taking notes, not so much on the overall discussions but mine were questions that I was too embarrassed to ask and would have to be explained in private by my very tolerant husband. As with any convention of this type, there was a "Trade Show" with many booths for absolutely anything and everything connected with ranching. There were computer programs which only needed to be added to one's personal computer, feed companies were touting their products as were the drug companies, Semen producers were selling semen for artificial insemination and a ranch equipment company were giving away white about a five feet long fiber glass cattle herding sticks with blue tips. I got one of these, not really knowing at that point what cattle I would be herding, but it was free and why not get one for future use.

When we finally started ranching, this stick was used many times. It does not hurt the animals. The funny part of this was, as I was walking through the airport in Dallas on the way home, I heard this one woman say to her companion, "I have never seen so many blind people in one spot." You must realize this was before security became so strict because I am sure I would or could not carry this object through any airport at this time.

One important booth was that of Lee Leachman who was promoting crossbreeding which was exactly what we were planning on doing. He had a picture of a *Salers* cow so we were asking him about that breed. From our preliminary studies, we thought we might be interested in the *Salers* as one of the breeds. He even had a live *Salers* cow in his booth for everyone to see. As we observed the cow, she became nervous and restless. His comment was, "This breed does not produce animals with good dispositions." Art and I just looked at each other and said, "Mark that breed off our list!" We left him and continued looking. The more people we spoke with, the more confused we got. But when all was said and done, most people said, "What you want is an Angus and Hereford cross. This combination produces the best replacements for cattle herds. Also, this combination will get you the best market price."

A decision was made. We will use Black Angus cows and Hereford bulls. Now to find just the right animals for the combination. Greg, our son, who fortunately has his Grandfather Chris's eye for picking cattle, as well as being on the Purdue University Livestock Judging team, along with his father, would be the choice makers. Certainly not me! I was still trying to learn all the different classifications of the female cows. Finally, father and son went to Gering, Nebraska to the ranch of Del Merritt, a fraternity brother of Arts while at the University of Nebraska. Del had purchased 450 bred heifers in South Dakota for resale. From this group, thirty-six heifers were purchased through a "gate cut" meaning the first animals through the gate would be the ones put in the trailer. However, my men spotted one which was especially attractive to them so she was allowed to be added to the group as a "Special." She will be mentioned later in the book as Number 25. Heifers are purchased, now the only thing needed was delivery to the ranch in Colorado.

The new year of 1993 was upon us. The barn was ready, but were we? Only time will tell! The day finally arrived in early February and a big truck pulling a huge cattle trailer came down the road. When the driver got out of the cab, he said, "Dad said you might want to watch these 37 girls as five of them could have their calves at any time." Panic! What did he mean? What were we supposed to look for and if we saw something, what were we supposed to do?

Our first delivery of cows in early February would change our lives. Of the 37 girls, five of them were ready to deliver.

I was standing by the truck and trailer as these beautiful creatures were being unloaded and suddenly realized I knew almost ABSOLUTELY NOTHING about cows. I knew that these particular creatures getting out of the trailer were identified as "Black Angus." Since I enjoy doing research, I wanted to know more about their history. Using *Breeds of Cattle* by Herman Purdy, R. John Dawes and Dr. Robert Hough as a resource, I found that the Angus breed began in the neighboring regions of Aberdeenshire and Angus in northeastern Scotland in 1523. After a period of time, the Scottish farmers realized this breed would best be utilized as producers of meat. Although very commonplace in the British Isles, this bred was introduced in the United States in 1873 when George Grant brought four Angus bulls to Victoria, Kansas to be used for crossbreeding with the already established breeds of Shorthorns and Longhorns. Here again, the local farmers noticed the good qualities of these bulls which led to importation of both sexes. By the early 1900s commercial cattlemen in the western states were looking to improve their herds so learning from the early thinking of the Scots, the Angus were chosen. This reasoning has been passed down from generation to generation and was considered by both of us when starting our herd. The heifers being unloaded had been bred by Angus bulls which meant the offspring would be polled (without horns) and would produce lower birth weight calves, which is desired especially in "first calf heifers." Most important would be the early maturation of the bull calves who would be a good size when going into a feedlot, thereby producing meat for marketing. The American Angus Association, in 1978 established a criteria for the evaluation of each animal thereby promoting the high quality of meat produced by this breed. When this is met, the meat will be labeled "Certified Angus Beef" which is noted by the local grocers in the meat counters.

I did not know that a cow (male or female) is classified as a "ruminant" or a cud chewing animal who has a very unique digestive system. I knew that it was a hoofed animal with beautiful long eyelashes and that it had four stomachs.

The cows' mouth has teeth only on the bottom jaw but with the aid of the tongue wrapping around plants or supplied forage (hay) the animals are able to consume the needed nutrients. The cow will eat the forage taking from 25,000 to 40,000 bites a day. The eaten forage will combine with saliva and the cow will continue chewing it enough to enable her to swallow it. When she is finished grazing and resting, the original forage (cud) that had not been completely chewed will be regurgitated from the rumen (first stomach). All the time the cud chewing is going on, the bacteria in the rumen are digesting the forage. Rumensin, a feed additive for cattle was discovered and developed by Art's research team at Eli Lilly. This discovery alters the bacterial process allowing the cow to obtain 10% more energy from the feed she consumes while reducing methane production by 30 - 40%. A mature cow has a rumen capacity of thirty to forty gallons of fluid. In this compartment, bacteria digest plant fibers allowing ruminants to thrive on grasses and hay. When the forage becomes liquid enough, it flows into the reticulum, a small area that collects hardware and other things a cow might dangerously ingest. This is why ranchers must be extremely careful when erecting fences that they do not leave pieces of wire laying on the ground. Even though the ranchers may not see it, it is possible a cow might eat it leading to disaster for the animal. The third stomach is the omasum which removes water from the ingesta, the fourth and final compartment, the abomasum, is the true stomach functioning like humans. In this compartment, acids and enzymes degrade food stuffs such as corn and oats (protein and carbohydrates). It also digests all the bacteria mass that was generated in the rumen. MOST IMPORTANT: Only ruminants can convert plants and grasses into human food.

I knew the animals in the trailer were heifers and had been chosen because they would be calving in late February or early March. Spring calving is preferred by many ranchers as it is favorable for both cow and calf. The spring grasses provide the nutrition needed for maximum milk production which increases for about the first four weeks. The cow produces twenty-five pounds of milk per day which equals four gallons at peak production. At about six weeks after birth the milk production starts to decline. The calves will continue nursing until they are weaned at about six months. By that time, the calf is joining mom in eating the hay provided by the ranchers or the natural grass growing in the pasture. Over the six-month period the calf will gain almost three pounds per day. Heifers having their first calf will produce significantly less milk than the older cows so every now and then a calf will be seen snitching milk from an older cow.

So much to learn and to do as now there were animals on the ranch that needed food, water and loving care. Following the trucker's advice about "watching for upcoming births" we took turns watching day and night. Watch we did! During the day, I would put a high "captain's chair" in front of my "window on the world" in the bedroom of the barn. From here I could observe the cows in the corral. I watched so much that my eyes had rings around them from holding the binoculars so tight. I was afraid I might miss the event if I were to put the glasses down for just a quick moment. I did, at one time, have second thoughts to myself, "What are we getting ourselves into?" But just standing next to these beautiful creatures and being able to actually touch them was a wonderful and exciting experience.

At night, armed with a flashlight Art would go to the corral every two hours to check on the heifers. He got the night duty as he could get dressed, go out, check the animals, come back in, take his coat off and immediately fall asleep. For me, doing the night duty, meant frequently putting on a complete set of warm clothes and boots because, after all, it was February in Colorado. Now this was not just an ordinary warm coat, no, it was a very warm Carhartt coat, possibly with a hood. Also needed was a pair of heavy Carhartt overalls, jeans, sweatshirt, gloves, and a stocking cap. Oh, yes! There were also the HEAVY BOOTS, better known as Sorrels. For those of you who have seen "The Christmas Story" remember the little boy that is all dressed for the snow and falls down and can't get up? Well, this is definitely how I felt each time I had to put on the armor and there is no going fast to anywhere when it is almost impossible to move.

Before knowing exactly what to watch for and what to do if we saw something, we had to experience the first birth. Five days after the arrival of the cows, and after days and nights of intensive watching, a cow was finally in labor. She was brought into the barn, put into a pen that had the floor covered with straw. There was a tub of grain and she had her own supply of water. We could do nothing but watch. "Oh, my gosh!" All of a sudden, the cow laid down and let out a "Mooooo!" Voila! A beautiful baby heifer calf was suddenly on the ground in a bed of straw. Mama got up, turned around, bent her head down and started licking the calf—all this time making soft sounds and probably telling her baby, "What a beautiful baby you are."

Eagles Nest's first baby is born and she truely was a beautiful baby.

When the baby was cleaned to the mother's satisfaction, it tried to stand up. "Oh, my gosh." "Look at that." First the front legs and then all of a sudden it went "PLOP." Trying again, first the front legs and finally the back ones. "OK, I am up, now what am I supposed to do?" All the time the mother was "Mooooing" quietly and probably saying "You're doing fine and it will get better!" All of a sudden, the baby was up on all fours so mama was ready to go to the next step. She did this by using her nose to push the calf around to her back side where the calf could nurse. This was not always successful but mama was patient so eventually the awestruck onlookers would hear a "slurp, slurp, slurp!" When the slurping stopped, the calf laid down and went sound to sleep. Mama also laid down as close to the baby as she could. She stayed there for a while and then got up and started giving her baby another bath. We were so excited. The first calf was successfully on the ground. Since we had only produced male babies, our sons, it was only appropriate to send out birth announcements saying "Our girl has finally arrived." So, there would be no misunderstanding, a picture of the calf was included. Just as a side note this mother was given the number 1, and went on to produce sixteen calves and was transported to and from Nebraska fifteen times covering a total of about 12,000 miles. She was eighteen years old when she left the herd.

"OK, I'm up, sort of." Calf number one stands for the first time.

Everything went well for the first few days when all of a sudden, a heifer was in labor but the feet were coming out upside down. PANIC! Call the vet, Dr. Woody Smith. "Please hurry!" We knew we had to get the cow in the head gate so everything would be ready when the vet got here. He was not far away so arrived in short order. He proceeded to show and tell us what to do. A veterinarian friend and co-worker at Eli Lilly had sent us a set of OB chains and handles just as a joke. Little did he know they would be put to use almost immediately. Since this was another lesson to be learned, both of us watched closely as the chains were wrapped around the calf's hooves which meant feeling inside the cow's reproductive tract for both legs of the calf. Woody using both sets of chains and handles quickly and carefully pulled the slippery baby out. Another "Oh, my gosh" moment. He then moved the baby around to the front of the mother. Her head was released from the previously mentioned head gate and she immediately went about the task of cleaning the baby. So, all was well. The funny part of this story is that after delivering the calf, the three of us went into the apartment and while we were having coffee and talking, two young mothers delivered their babies outside in the corral without any help and without anyone watching.

Calving was going well until we decided to go into town to celebrate Valentine's Day. When we got to the main road and looked into the pasture, there was a cow with her head down. There was a baby on the ground in front of her. So much for being dressed up. Back to the barn to change clothes and out to the pasture to bring mom and baby into the barn as the night would be cold. This time Art got the baby into the back of the "red pickup truck" then he got in, holding the calf in plain view of the mother. I drove the truck slowly, all the time watching making sure the mom was following. It was learned quite early that if the cow cannot see her calf being transported either by being carried by a human or being transported by a vehicle (truck, wheel barrow or wagon) she will return to where the calf had been born not realizing it is her baby being moved to the barn. We were successful in getting both animals into the barn on our first try. We later bought a wagon with heavy duty tires that had see through wire panels and would navigate through a muddy corral. This made moving the new born much easier as the wagon was closer to the ground and Art would not have to lift it as high as he had to when using the truck or wheelbarrow. It also made it easier for the mother to see her calf as she would be walking behind the wagon.

Sometimes the cows like to trick the humans. Even though Art would be checking them every two hours all night long, the cows will have their calves when they are ready PERIOD! "Ooops! What is that sound?" "Wake Up, I think we have a calf." After giving birth the mother will moo and since our animals were spoiled, they did not moo often so when they did—you take notice. Both of us now became bona fide ranchers as we would get up, put on the armor and take the wheelbarrow out to the corral. All the mothers and babies are kept in the barn or shed for a couple of days until there's enough to safely put them in a small corral. As the numbers increase, all the pairs will be turned out to a separate pasture just for moms and new born.

After the moms and their new born calves leave the barn, each pen is completely cleaned by first removing and sweeping out all the straw bedding. A liquid soap is applied and the pen completely washed out. (Each pen has its own water supply). The pen is then rinsed with a solution of bleach water and left to dry. When completely dry, a bale of straw will be spread out and ready for the next occupant.

When the moms and calves were in the pasture, it was time to put the good old red truck to use again. Now instead of fence and building materials, it carried fifty-pound bales of hay. I was in charge of driving this stick shift machine and was told many times, "Slow Down," as Art was in the back throwing the bales off to the hungry mothers and any jerking motion could be disastrous. (Just another lesson to be learned.) One interesting observation by me was that it didn't take long for the calves to find the hay. It would be a while before they would start eating it, but it sure was a soft place to lay and to take a quick nap while their mothers were busy eating around them.

May it be assumed that by now the experienced ranchers are laughing at our antics. The ranches in the western states will have hundreds of cows. This entails having many ranch hands who will be caretakers of possibly one hundred or more cows. Although they are equally concerned about each animal, they are not able to provide as much individual attention as do the owners of small herds. Our herd is small (37- 60) and could be considered a "Hobby" by others, but no matter what it is called, ranching of any size is nature at its best.

The calves will always find a spot to lie in the hay while their mom's graze around them.

WHO'S WHO IN THE BOVINE WORLD

With the arrival of the first calf, we realized we needed a system by which we could immediately match the calf with the correct mother. This was not easy as all the cows were black and so were the calves making them all look alike to this city girl. We had looked at some profession computer record systems, but not doing exactly what we wanted, we made our own. Date, time, place of birth, weight and sex was all we needed. The second year, because of the cross breeding with a Hereford bull, we added color, such as all black or black/white face. The animals, both cow and calf are given an ear tag with an identification number causing a little girl to ask, "Why do the babies have price tags in their ears?"

The numbering system includes the year of birth so the first cow to deliver was given

These are not "price tags" in their ears, they are numbers used for identification.

the number 9101 meaning she was born in 1991. Her calf was given the number 9301 as the first two numbers were the year and the last two were the same last two of her mothers. On the back of the ear tag is marked the exact date of her birth, 2/14. If the calf is a female to be used as a replacement for Eagles Nest Ranch, she will be given a new cow number at weaning. Her old number will be noted on the back of the tag along with her birth date. This is all recorded in the ranch pedigree book, showing the ancestry of the cow which prevents any inbreeding. It is my job to make the tags and record details in our record book. Sometimes it gets a little confusing because Art and I have cows and so do Tim and Greg. To differentiate owners, Art's and my tags are yellow, Greg's are orange and Tim's are blue. When Art and I are working together in the field checking on the animals, we must be very careful and call out colors as well as numbers as there are some identical numbers in the herd. It makes life very interesting!

Ranchers with large herds quite probably do not do this but since this is a small operation, it was a way to always know who belongs to whom and also make sure the calf was nursing on the right cow and not snitching from someone else. This really does happen. This is quite interesting because it usually happens when the correct calf is nursing on either side of the cow and the snitch comes up from behind, sticking its head between the back legs of the cow, preventing the cow from being able to see or side kick the calf. How about that for tricking the mom?

When the heifers (female calves) are about seven months old, they are given a brucellosis vaccination (bangs vaccination). This is a very serious disease that the government has effectively eradicated nationwide and the vaccination is only administered by a certified veterinarian. This disease can be passed to humans mainly though the consumption of unpasteurized dairy products. When administered, a tattoo is put in the right ear as well as a metal tag with a number, identifying this individual animal. This number will never be used again and is recorded by the owners as well as the veterinarian. These tags and numbers are used for identification and proof of vaccination when the animals are sold or moved from one state to another. If the metal tag is lost, which does happen, a replacement tag/number is recorded but the vaccination does not need to be repeated.

Naming the Calves

One question asked frequently is, "Do your calves have names?" "No, not usually, but there have been exceptions."

The first ones to be given names were Samantha and Norma. They were two calves who had bloated stomachs. Because it was early spring with the mothers eating fresh green grass and producing a lot of milk, it was thought this might have led to the more serious calf problems. To solve the situation, it was decided both calves would become "bottle babies" so that milk consumption could be continued. To do this meant filling two-quart bottles (one designed especially for this purpose) with a milk substitute, or formula as would be given to humans. The calves were fed three times a day, spoiling them as well, so they were given names Samantha and Norma. Their tags showed their numbers, not their names. Over time, as the calves grew, they came to know their names and when it was time for their bottles, I would stand at the barn door and call them. If they were within hearing distance, they would answer with a "Moo" and come running. As this procedure continued, it eventually was changed to self-feeding as the bottles were put in receptacles hanging on the fence so they could drink at will. It was always a treat for the young visitors when they got to feed Samantha and Norma. Many photos of people of all ages were taken of this operation.

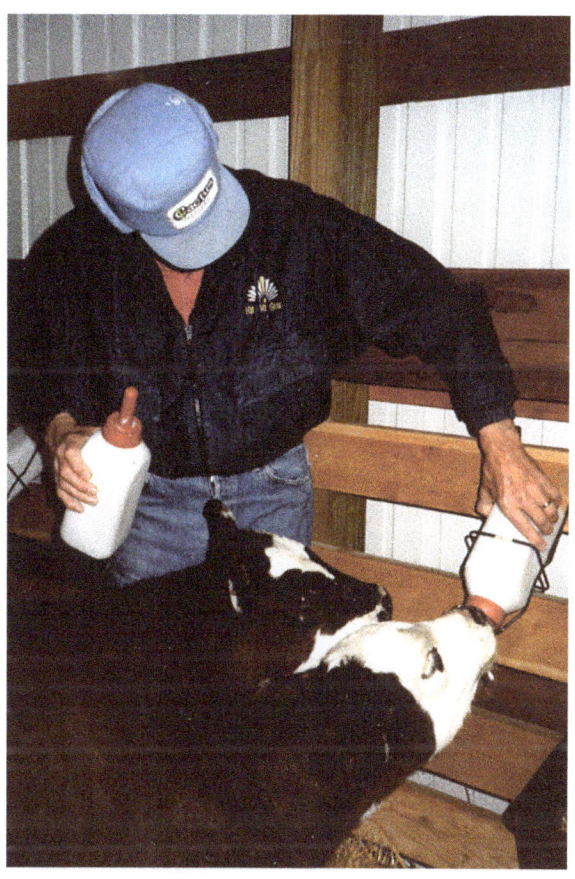

Art bottle-feeding Samantha and Norma. Bottle-fed for health reasons, they would come running when their names were called.

There was another "Sam" but this time it was because he was born on Sunday A.M. Sam was the first born in a set of twins born in the pasture. He was found all by himself, quite probably where the mother had delivered. He was all cleaned up so the mother knew she had given birth but then went off to another spot to deliver the second calf. This is not unusual for a cow having twins to forget she already had the first one. After a couple of tries, we were able to determine the identity of the mother and tried to put the first born at her side. Unfortunately, she wanted no part of this so Sam was put in the back of the Excursion, driven to the barn and put in a pen filled with clean straw. He was then given a milk solution containing colostrum, a source of antibodies which are important for the first few weeks of the calf's life. Sam became another bottle baby and while growing rapidly, he became a pet. He had free run of the area around the barn but would usually hang out in a grassy area by the barn. He knew his bottle came from inside the apartment, so if the door was accidently left open, Sam would bolt in. His visits inside the apartment were the subject of that year's Christmas card picture. When Sam was about six weeks old, the ranchers had a calf die unexpectedly. In such cases, it is not unusual to take the hide from the dead calf and tie it over a live one that has been orphaned. The cows identify their calves by smell and as far as we know, the calves identify their mothers by her moo. This procedure convinced the cow that Sam was her calf but Sam had never nursed a mother so had to be taught. This was done by putting the mom in the head gate and helping Sam find the udder. After many tries, it was successful and Sam liked what he was getting. It was decided to put mama and Sam in a pen, thinking he could do it on his own. No such luck! So back to the head gate with Sam on the other side of the cow. Eventually, Sam figured it out, got a full belly, the cow got relief and the adoption was a success.

Then there was Excursion! Excursion had accidentally been left behind in Nebraska when her mom was trucked to Colorado in the spring. Before loading the cows in Nebraska, Art repeatedly asked the farm hands, "Are you SURE there are no cows with calves in this trailer?" They were quite positive but when this one cow

Granddaughter Katie feeding Sam, the twin who was left by his mother and needed a helping hand.

got out of the trailer in Colorado, she immediately started calling for her calf. She bellowed all night and by morning it was decided Art would take the Ford Excursion back to Nebraska, making a 700-mile round trip, and have the calf back by nightfall. There was already a rubber mat in the back of the car and the make-shift wire cage would fit nicely to keep the calf in place. Art went off, expecting to find a small, possibly a week-old calf but what a surprise he got when the calf was probably a month old and quite active. With help, Art got the calf in the cage. The calf apparently enjoyed the scenery as she stood up for most of the entire six-hour trip. She finally laid down for about the last hour of the trip. Art said he drove with "one eye on the road and the other on his passenger in the back." When the car stopped at the barn, the mother was on the other side of the fence, waiting for her baby. Shortly after opening a gate, the two were quickly united. What a happy reunion for both!

I wrote to the Ford Magazine who are interested in publishing personal experiences, "We have two Excursions, one with four wheels and the other with four legs." This was published for all to read. Excursion was a pure-bred Angus and remained productive mother cow in the herd, giving us many calves over the years.

When the heifers were first being looked at in Nebraska, there was one that Art and Greg thought was exceptional so she was added to the initial 37. The heifer was the 25th animal to give birth and while she was never actually named, she became known as "The Cube Eater." Was she more intelligent than the rest of the heifers? Probably not, but maybe it was because she was more interested in the cubes being put in the creep feeder. At first, she stood by the red pickup watching Art as he shoveled the pellets of calf creep feed into the self-feeder with a cage around it which only the calves can get into. Heifer #25 watched him do this a few times and then he would turn, giving her a bit of the feed. She, very quickly, realized Art was the source of her feed and whenever the pickup was in the pasture, she would instantly be at Art's side looking for her treat. This went on for quite a spell. As time went on, she started bumping the edge of the bag. Of course, this made the feed hit the ground where she would clean it up. Art took a chance and put some of the feed in his hand, holding it out for "our girl" to see. From that day on, she became our "Cube Eater." As I have said before, cows are nosey so when other heifers saw what was happening, they apparently thought, "If she can get special treatment, why can't I." Gradually others would come around.

If we hold out our hand with a cube on it, they might take a look, and usually back away. Gradually more and more would gather around for their treats so now it is a tradition. When visitors are here, small or large groups, treats are carried to the pasture and the cows come running. They know they will be getting treats. Many of the cows will eat from the visitor's hand which results in comments such as, "The cow wrapped its tongue completely around my hand and it felt like sand paper!" Some of the younger, and not as nosey, cows will still stand back but as the visitors are being driven away, the left-over treats are spread on the ground. This keeps the cows from following the truck and wagon, plus the ones that had not been brave enough, may partake of the left overs.

Now we have #90 who is also a cube eater. When I go to the pasture on foot or in the Gator, she is always looking for cubes. If I don't have any, after she has already checked my hands and smelled my pockets, I say, "Sorry girl. I didn't bring any today." She sort of gives me a disappointed look and will walk away giving me a slight bump with her hip. Our animals are definitely spoiled, loved and properly cared for.

Naming the Bulls

Naming bulls is different as they are registered animals so unique names are given at birth and recorded, the same as humans. The names are a part of their pedigree and retained by ranchers who purchase them. This cannot be changed and always stay with that one animal. The pure-bred black Hereford bulls all have registered names, such as ENA Cory Thor 2099, whose father's name is JRK 258 Special Thor 543, and his grandfather's name is JRK 220 Cory Thor 543 714. Each animal is duly registered with the American Black Hereford Association.

When bulls are born at the Eagles Nest Ranch, they cannot be registered as the cows are considered "commercial cows." They will respond by perking up their ears when I call out "Hey, bully, bully!" Eventually they look around and then go back to whatever they were doing—probably eating!

THE MIRACLE OF NEW LIFE

Bringing Cows to the Corral

One question often asked is, "How do you know when to bring the cows into the corral to be closely watched?" The cows are closely looked at each morning when they are fed in the pasture with notations made for future use. Once in the corral, the cows are watched continuously and the following signs are noted.

    1. Swollen vulva
    2. Tail head sticking up because the mussels in her back are relaxing
    3. Her utter is tight and looking full
    4. Reliable breeding date in record book, determined by AI date and visual servicing by the bull

Birthing Procedure

A frequently asked question, especially by women, is, "What is the gestation period for cows?" It is nine months or 283 days which may vary a bit from humans but only by a couple of days. How do you know when the cow is about to calve?

1. The cow will likely go out by herself, away from the others in the herd.
2. She will be pacing, walking around and around while sniffing the ground, looking for a place to have the calf.
3. Her tail will be out, sometimes with sort of a crook in it. Hard to describe but definitely a sign.
4. She will be restless, laying down and getting up frequently. She will not be happy in either position.

5. She will be licking and kicking at her sides.
6. Some placenta fluid and tissues will be released.
7. Seeing hooves of the calf is definitely a good sign. However, they may be seen and then go back in a number of times but when they are fully observed, the cow will lay down and start pushing in earnest. If the hooves are pointing to the ground, it means everything should be OK. If the cow seems to be having a problem and needs assistance, she will be put in the barn in the head gate. A strong person will wrap a chain around the pastern on both legs (what would be like a human wrist) and this chain would be attached to a handle and now you wait for the cow to have a contraction, at which time you pull.

We were at a Calf/Cow Symposium sponsored by Colorado State University where I was trying to learn more about cattle and I asked cattle woman from Wyoming, "How do you know when to pull?" Her answer was, "Women are better at this than men because women will feel the cow's contraction." As a result, if I am standing by when the pulling is being done, I will say, "Wait a minute" and fortunately, the men will listen.

If the hooves are pointing up, this means the calf will be coming out backwards (breech) and needs to be pulled immediately. The reason being that when the calf is halfway out the umbilical cord is pinched off causing the calf to suffocate.

Normally the cow will deliver the calf without any problems but we carefully watch each mother and will be on standby if help is needed. We will not let the cow be in labor for more than two hours. If labor time is extended, the cow could get so physically worn out she would not have the stamina to immediately tend to her calf. Under normal conditions when the calf is released, the cow will stand up, turn around and begin licking her baby. When she is satisfied that the calf has been properly cleaned, she will use her nose under the butt of the calf helping the calf get up and in position to nurse. After a few failed attempts, the calf will be steady enough to find the udder. The cow will lick the butt of the calf, stimulating it to nurse. When the whole procedure is deemed a success, both mother and baby will lay down and take a long nap.

Experiences During Calving

"Hurry up and wait," is an expression quite often used but is especially true during calving season. From March to the middle of May, we live in the apartment in the barn so we can watch the cows either in the corrals or in the barn pens, making sure the birthing procedure was going well. During this time, we play Scrabble or Yatzee or maybe, even Bridge.

Playing Bridge is hard when there are only two people but we are fortunate to have neighbors, Vern and Nancy, who live only twenty miles away (in rural Colorado, that is close). Once a week these friends would bring dinner or take not "pot luck" but "luck of the pot" since I am somewhat short on cooking utensils or a real stove with an oven in the barn. A running score sheet is kept for the season and a final score tallied. Most of the time it is pretty even but once in a while, the conservative women bidders will be lucky, so from the women's standpoint, we were by far the better players. Of course, this could be argued!

Sometimes the Bridge game would be interrupted by a noise from a pen in the barn meaning a calf was in the process of being born or had already hit the ground. At any rate, everyone present goes out to check on the activity. After this special event, the Bridge game is put aside and the humans stand to watch the mother do her job of cleaning off the baby. When this has been accomplished, the mother proudly presented her beautiful baby to the onlookers.

"It's a little chilly out here," says a new-born calf.

Help Needed

One night, as we were watching a cow in the barn, we realized she was going to need help. I was recovering from recent surgery so could not be of any help. This time a young neighboring couple, Kris and Patrice, were called. "We need help. Can you come right away?" It seemed as if they were at the door even before the phone had been put down. Kris was given rubber gloves, Art put the chains around the calf's hooves and both men, using the handles on the chains, quickly pulled the calf who landed on a tarp at their feet. What makes this incident so memorable is that Patrice was eight and one-half months pregnant with their first child. Her comment after watching this whole amazing birthing process was, "I hope my delivery goes better than this did!" It did and they have a beautiful daughter.

The Urgent Phone Call

One other time, always at night, the cow had been in labor over two hours and only one leg was showing—definitely a sign that help was needed! Art had been watching this cow over the closed-circuit TV while she was in the shed but knowing help was needed, Art got her into the barn and caught her in the head gate. Upon examination, Art realized the other leg was turned backwards. He then said, "I am not strong enough to get the leg turned" so what to do? It was getting late. Past nine o'clock is late as morning comes early in cattle country. The vet was called but no one answered. A message was left but no return call was received. Greg had just had a Chemo infusion and definitely not in a position to pull a calf. However, there was one person who over the years had said, "If you ever need help, please call me." Jim Faughnan was called and his answer was, "I'll be right there." He lived about ten miles from the ranch and came immediately, taking his coat off as he came through the barn door. Being raised as a rancher and being much taller and stronger than either Art or Greg, he was definitely the person to call. He put on the plastic glove, with a sleeve long enough to reach a person's shoulder and examined the cow's birth canal. After what seemed like an eternity, he turned to the ranchers and said, "I have turned the leg. The calf is still alive. Let's use the 'Come Along' and carefully extract the calf." (The "Come Along" is a long steel rod with a bar that goes under the cows' butt and a chain that is placed over her back to hold everything else in place. Further down the rod are large hooks which will hold the chains, which have been wrapped around the hooves of the calf. When this is accomplished, there is a handle that sort of acts like a jack and using it will safely and slowly deliver the calf. It is not inhuman to use, but it is something that would rather not be used, except in dire circumstances—which this was. All things considered; a beautiful black Hereford bull was delivered. The calf is now named ENA Cory Thor 2099 and will remain part of the herd as an active bull.

The three of us were so fortunate and thankful to have Jim as a neighbor and a friend but isn't that what it is all about? As Jim was going out the door, he turned and said, "When the phone rang at eleven o'clock, I knew someone needed help." WOW! WHAT A FRIEND!

Twins

This was one of those "Oh, my gosh" days. Art had gone to Nebraska to bring the last load of pregnant cows home, leaving me to tend to the ranch. I drove to the barn in the morning, only to find two cows had given birth during the night. Both calves were up and nursing so all was well. The only problem was that "Storm Warnings" had been issued with snow arriving at 3:30 p.m. I relayed this information to Art who replied confidently, "I'll be home by then." OK. I took up my post at my "window on the world" and watched as a cow delivered a calf. That went well. The calf was thoroughly cleaned, was up and nursing, so no worries, except the time was creeping closer to the 3:30 deadline.

It got to be noon, so I called Art asking his location. Not good! He was still in Nebraska, at least four hours away. He asked me to go to the town of Elizabeth, fifteen miles away, to the Big R store and pick up a couple of bales of straw. Which I did, but returning to the barn and looking over at the newest mom, I saw two calves. Oh. My gosh! There were no other cows in sight, which meant this one had twins. This time it was a frantic call to Art. "We've got twins" and "Where are you?" "That's great and I am in Kansas." Once again, this was not good as the storm was fast approaching. It was starting to rain. Art calmly said, "I will call you from Limon (45 miles from the ranch) to check on road conditions. Coming the usual way from Limon to Elbert involves navigating two sections of long, high hills. Art was pulling a cattle trailer loaded with 15,000 pounds of cows and if the road conditions were bad, it would be treacherous to say the least. The other option was to drive approximately twenty miles further, on relatively flat roads, avoiding the hills. Either way, my dear husband would not be home before 3:30.

Identical Twins born in 2019. Numbers 75 A and 75 B grew to be beautiful with their mother doing a terrific job.

    By the time Art got home it was starting to snow a very wet snow and the new born calves were getting wet, and with a drop in temperature, they needed to be put in the dry shed. Together, we went out to see the new born calves and Art said, "I'll get the Excursion and we can put the babies in the back. We'll leave the car doors open, so the mom will see them. She will follow as we drive them to the shed." Only one problem, the back of the Excursion was filled with baled straw that I had picked up earlier as I had been asked to do. (Such a good and faithful wife.) I stayed out in the pasture, making sure the mother and babies would stay put until they could be successfully moved to the shed. All of a sudden, I heard this "Rooooooar" and looking up, there was Art driving the tractor through the corral, down the hill, through the creek bed, up the hill and stopping at the birthing site. He lowered the bucket on the front of the tractor, climbed down from his seat and said, "I'll put some straw in the bucket and we'll put one calf on one side, the other on the other side, and you will sit in the middle, holding both of them from falling out." Oh, my gosh! This sounded like quite a plan but I do not like heights, let alone trying to keep two lively calves from falling out from the raised bucket. But we got loaded and off we went! Driving backwards down the hill so the cow could see the calves, Art went through the creek bed, up the hill before stopping at the corral fence. At this time, the bucket was raised even higher in order to get over the fence on either side of the corral gate, but all was going well. Luckily, apparently enjoying the ride, the calves did not move and mother cow was following as was hoped. When reaching the destination, I climbed out of the bucket, feeling rather weak in the knees, ran to the barn for towels to dry off the calves before putting them in the dry shed where bedding had already been placed. Mission accomplished. Let the snow come!

All's well that ends well! Calf numbers 75 A and 75 B grew to be beautiful calves, with the cow doing a terrific job of parenting.

Another set of twins, one red and white and the other black and white.

Breech Baby

One story I like to tell is about when a group of six and seven-year-old children were brought to the ranch to see the cows and the new born calves. When it is known that a group of youngsters are coming, we will keep a new born in the barn so the children can pet it. Their comments are always the same, "The coat is so soft." But this day was different. As the children arrived, an expectant cow was put in the alley leading to the barn where she would go to deliver her calf. I asked the parents if it was alright for the children to observe the birthing process. All agreed that it would be fine. The cow was not quite ready to deliver so the children and adults were put on the flatbed truck and taken out to the pasture. Here they would see the calves and also give the cows some treats. When returning to the barn, I noticed there were two legs protruding from the birth canal of the cow. This was not good because they were the back legs which meant a breech birth. I ran one way while Art ran the other, each knowing what we were to do. My job was to put water in a pail with some disinfectant along with the OB chains and handles to be used when pulling the calf. Art was bringing the cow into the barn and would catch her in the head gate. The guests followed into the barn and stood off to the side, close enough to the operation to get a good view. They stood there so very quietly, watching and listening as I was explaining what we were doing. Most important was telling them that the cow was not being hurt. Fortunately, the operation went well. A beautiful calf was born ALIVE! She landed on a tarp placed on the floor behind the cow. The new born is so slippery that putting them on the tarp makes it easier to move them around to be by the mothers' head. Art opened the head gate releasing the cows' head and immediately, the mom starting licking her baby. All the time, I was explaining the guttural and the very soft "mooing" sounds the cow was making as if she was talking to her baby. The children watched, listened and none seemed in the least bit frightened. The cow and calf were moved into a pen where I was explaining how the cow would continue licking and then use her nose to help get the calf up and nursing. When everything was in place, we all went into the apartment so the children could eat their lunch. Now, they were full of questions. One little girl asked, "When I'm a mom, will I know what to do?' I answered, "Of course, you will." I found out later that two of the little girls were playing 'breech baby" with the cloth cow dolls from Chick-Fil-A. How about that for a learning example?

Cow Chase

Calving time is full of new experiences making for good stories. In Colorado, most days have beautiful blue cloudless skies but this one day was chilly, not really cold, but cold enough for humans to be wearing coats. There was one cow in the east pasture, about to have a calf so Art said, "Let's take her to the shed." He had already thought about this and had a pen waiting for her. He got behind her, getting her into the first corral, then on through the first set of gates. From here on is where things got interesting. One of the people gates leading into the barn had been left open. The cow saw her chance to escape which she did! She walked through the gate, through the alley, into and through the barn, ending up in the wide open space of the pasture. She turned and walked close to the side of the barn. Thinking she could be captured at the next set of gates, I followed her. Unfortunately, none of the those gates were open. The cow kept walking west down the fence line with Art following and me trying to sneak around to get ahead of her. This did not work. She left the fence line, walked up a steep hill, so steep Art had to abandon the Gator. He got off and tried to catch up with the cow but to no avail. She kept on walking, coming to the driveway where she took off walking north now going up another hill. I had gotten into the car and had driven north part way up the driveway. Getting out of the car, I started chasing the cow on foot. Clumsy me, I fell over a rock. This enabled the cow to get further away. I called Greg for help. By the time he joined the chase, the cow had reached the top of a hill and crossed a cattle guard into the southeast pasture. Art followed the cow, turning her onto an old cow path leading to the barn. If lucky, the cow would stay on that path, ending up back down at the barn. Greg and I went ahead, opening gates so when Art got her down the hill, the route to the shed would be open. This procedure went well. Once the cow passed through one gate, it would be closed so she could not escape again. Through another couple of gates, the runaway cow was now completely restrained. Into the shed she went. Mission Accomplished! Well, not exactly. Once in the pen she must have decided this was not where she really wanted to be. Being rather restless she started trying to open the closed gate by bumping it numerous times. Apparently, she wanted a little more room. After all, she had just experienced a mile long hike in the wide-open spaces. Greg opened the gate to the pen and then closed one that would have taken her to a corral. She needed to be in a small area as the two hooves were already showing which meant birthing would come soon. She spent a short period of time walking in and out of the pen and finally she walked into the clean pen, laid down and within seconds presented the three of us onlookers with a black white-faced bull calf.

We certainly had our exercise for the day, not to mention the cow had certainly taken us not on a "wild goose chase" but a "pregnant cow chase!"

The Disappearing Cow

As it is with pregnant women, it is also with cows when it comes to when and where they want to deliver their baby. So, it was on this one spring day, Art was feeding large round bales of hay to the pregnant cows in the east pasture. As usual, I was riding side saddle on the tractor so I could open the gates and count the cows.

Before going to the field, we had put a pregnant cow in a pen in the barn because delivery was imminent. We fed the cows in the east pasture and before going to the west, I went in the barn to check on the cow and possibly a new calf. When I got there, not only was there not a new calf but there was no cow either. Apparently, the cow had used her head to jar the chains loose and with a push, got two gates open. I ran to the tractor and said, "The cow is gone!" Art answered, "What do you mean, the cow is gone?" "SHE IS GONE!" I declared with my hands squarely on my hips. Wherever could she be? So, for the next four hours, we drove over, walked over and with binoculars looked over every inch of the close by field. Finally, in desperation, we once again started out on foot. Art went up the hill toward the house and "Lo and Behold" here in a heavily wooded area was the cow with her new calf in a grassy clearing between two huge rocks and a few trees. After staring at each other for a split second, the cow, with her calf following proceeded to walk directly back to the barn where Art put her in the waiting pen. I can't say sure who was the smartest of the two—mother or human but that cow just did not want to have her baby in the barn. SO, THERE YOU ARE!

Ruth in a moment of quiet time feeding a calf, as this new-born was reluctant to nurse. All in a day's work.

PARTING IS SUCH SWEET SORROW

It was a sad day in December of 1993 when the steer calves were loaded into the cattle trailer to be sold at market. I stayed behind at the ranch not being able to watch them being sold and I even cried a bit. It was as if I was losing a dear friend or even a family member. I had watched these creatures from birth, through their "teen years" and now it was time for them to be on their own. Of course, not really on their own as none of us would speculate on their future. But then, always being an optimist, I looked to the future and the babies who would be arriving in March, April or May. The calves born in the spring of 1993 were all black since they were purebred Angus but from now on, the calves would be black with white faces. Some might have black spots around their eyes while others might have a small tip of white on their tails, all due to the fact that the male component is a brown and white Hereford bull. I could not stay sad long because we had an interesting future ahead of us. We would be watching the 1993 heifers which had been added to our herd, grow into motherhood. In 1995 they would be giving birth to their own offspring. After all, this is a business and nature's way. My new way of life is now to watch my babies be part of the cattle sale.

A cattle sale involving both buyers and sellers is held in a "Sale Barn." This barn is not a typical barn that one would see driving through the countryside. It is usually a large building with what would be considered a normal store front with doors and windows. What makes it a "Sale Barn" are the many pens in the adjacent yard outside. On cattle sale days these pens are filled with cattle of all sizes and colors. Other days, these pens could be filled with sheep, goats or even mules.

Inside the front door is a counter behind which are very busy people, mostly women, who register the ranchers who are selling their animals. There are others who are buying cattle for feed lots and need numbers for identification. (A feed lot is where the cattle go to be fed certain rations so they will gain between 600 and 700 pounds and to lay on some body fat before going to slaughter.) Most feed lots are located in Nebraska, Colorado, Kansas, and Texas.

Greg and Art checking in at the sale barn.

Before the sale, the women behind the counter are busy collating the "sale bill" listing all the animals to be sold that day. There will the history of each animal, such as birth weight, weaning weight, shot records as well as names of the owners or ranch where the cattle were raised. After the sale the women will be collecting the money from the buyers and distributing checks to the sellers. One day as I was watching the working women, I thought to myself, "These women hardly have time to take a break." I then decided that the next time we took cattle to the sale, I would make a coffee cake so the crew could at least have a snack, which I did. This was very welcomed and even the auctioneer thanked me from his post. I said "You weren't supposed to say anything" to which he replied, "It's too late now, it's all over the internet." (These sales are televised and buyers may bid and buy over the internet.) So much for privacy. Now when they know we are bringing cattle, they look forward to getting a coffee cake.

Also in the lobby is a Brand Inspector who makes sure the cattle actually belong to the person selling them. Next to him is the Health Inspector who checks the health certificate signed by the rancher's local veterinarian stating that the animals are healthy and have been cleared for sale.

The sale barn we go to is in Ogallala, Nebraska, a four-hour drive from the ranch. We chose this one because of the many feedlots in the region. We take the cattle to the facility the night before where they are put in one of the outside pens in the yard and recorded as cattle from the Eagles Nest Ranch. The next day before the sale actually begins, the prospective buyers will go to the yard and look over the animals thus giving them heads up to know which animals they want to buy.

After looking over all the pens, the sellers (if they are there) and buyers go into the crude arena, some have real chairs while others may have wide concrete steps which serve as seats. In the center of this room is a floor which covers a scale so when the cattle are brought in, their weight is recorded and divided by the number of occupants, thereby giving the average weight per animal. As many as 50 head of weaned 600-pound calves are brought in at one time. The number is less when full grown cows are being sold.

In front of the semi-circle of seats and a level above is where the auctioneer is seated, along with telephones, computers and at least five people manning the communications. Bidding is also done on the internet from distant regions. The auctioneer is the main person when the sale begins. He has knowledge of the animals being sold as well as the going prices for the day. He most generally starts by saying what a fine group of cattle is in the ring and then he starts with a price. To an outsider it sounds like a bit of gibberish but to the listening buyer, it is a price on which they may or may not bid. On the floor, in the semi-circle, are two men called "ring men," who along with the auctioneer and others in the box above are watching for signals from the prospective buyers. No matter how hard I try, it is almost impossible to tell who is bidding. It all goes very quickly and when the sale is completed, the auctioneer says "Open the gate" or "Let 'em out" at which time the big doors at one edge of the arena are opened and the group of cattle go out, being replaced by another group coming though doors on the other side. One important note: When attending a cattle sale in the summer months, the bystander needs to be careful not to swat flies or they may end up buying a pen of cattle!!

The sale goes on for many hours, sometimes even well into the night. As many as 9,000 cattle may be sold in one day. But not to worry! On one side of the lobby is a restaurant where simple but good food is prepared. Breakfast, lunch and dinner are served and there is always a supply of homemade pies topped with ice cream.

Prior to Sale Day

The day before the actual sale, the area outside is a flurry of activity. There are trucks with trailers of all sizes waiting to unload their cargo. Small ranchers, such as us, will have small trailers, holding from two to thirteen mature cows or twenty-five 600-pound calves. The large "potbellied" semi-trailers, because of their two decks in the middle of the trailer, can carry 45 mature cows or no more than a total weight of 55,000 pounds. These trailers are commercial haulers, often seen on the highway, with a company name proudly displayed on the front of the trailer. A ranch to be viable to support a family would have four to five hundred cows producing two hundred plus steers and two hundred plus heifers, so when they get ready to sell probably half of the herd would be sold as steers. Here is a case when a commercial hauler would be used to haul the animals to the sale barn. After the animals are sold, there will be another group of commercial haulers to take the feeder steers and heifers to the various feed lots found in Nebraska, Kansas, Colorado and Texas.

When the trailers arrive at the sale barn, the animals are unloaded and taken to a designated clean pen in the yard where there will be water and hay. They will stay in the pen until they are called for the sale. This smooth and very quiet operation is carried out by "cow" dogs of various breeds, as they move ahead of employees on horseback. When the sale is completed, the animals will be taken to another pen. The auctioneer will say, for example, "126 on 2" meaning the buyer is number 126 and 2 is the new pen. The buyer is possibly buying cattle for a number of feed lots so would have many pens. The purchases will depend on the size of his trailer and the total weight of the cattle.

The whole experience of the sale and sale barn is a hard procedure to describe but it is one that should surely be attended at least once in a lifetime. There are buyers, sellers, along with families and children waiting with anticipation to see how the sale of their special animal or animals is going. As for the occupants in the arena, they leave at the end of the day, tired and smelling as if they had been in cattle barn. In fact, they were.

Bull Sale

"Honey, there is a bull sale today," are words a spouse really does not want to hear. Although, quite prepared for this statement, because of the various catalogs that have been coming in the mail and are now covering the coffee table, the wife has two choices. She could pretend she didn't hear him, or she could say, "Where and when are WE going."

When a rancher has a large herd of what he considered "Prize Bulls" he will have photos taken and a catalog compiled with pertinent information on each animal. This will include the ancestry, actual birth weight, the weaning weight, usually 650 pounds or more, EPD's (Expected progeny difference) which means the expected performance of the offspring, and a yearling weight usually 950 pounds or above. The sale of these animals usually occurs in January or February so the animal will be available for spring breeding. With this type of sale, there is usually a day prior when perspective buyers can physically look over each animal. This is also a time of social activities, good food and storytelling. One such story involved a rancher who was observing a crop of fine-looking calves. He asked his wife which bull was the sire and she responded "number 10." This went on for a period of time, always with the wife answering, "number 10." Finally, the rancher said, "I don't remember buying Number 10" to which the wife replied, "You didn't. I did while you were in the rest room." At any rate, the wife will quite probably go along, having to endure possibly horrible weather and many muddy corrals, as the couple spend hour upon hours, walking from pen to pen, looking at back end of bulls-looking for the required necessities needed to produce perfect calves.

The other option for the wife is to stay at home and join hubby as he sits in front of the computer screen, watching as animals are paraded into the sale barn and the auctioneer goes about his business. Forget doing anything on the computer as it must be readily available if hubby wants to bid on number so and so, listed on page such and such. This procedure occurred one day when there was a sale going on in Dunning, Nebraska with Art at home in Colorado and Greg in Hawaii, both with eyes glued to the screen. Discussion of what type of bull was needed and the bidding price had been agreed upon. The criteria had been established by Greg, as he had been a livestock judge while in college at Purdue University. Here each judge looks at how the bull appears physically, muscling in the hind quarter, big body cavity, how the bull stands and walks because the number one problem with a bull is his feet which causes him to have trouble walking. Characteristics of his manly look are also evaluated. Selecting a bull that meets all of those criteria is very important as the bull passes these characteristics to all offspring in the herd while the cow determines the characteristics of only one or maybe two, if twins, calves.

Sitting in front of the computer screens, both Art and Greg were watching as the sale began with a going price of $20,000, much more than what Eagles Nest Ranch wanted to pay. They were wanting an animal that had a "low birth weight" suitable for breeding heifers and had picked five choices from the available catalog. The sale progressed with both men watching closely. Most of the bulls had been sold but Art and Greg's first choice had yet to enter the show ring. The prices had come down to the three-to-five-thousand-dollar range with Greg now watching even closer and Art was holding the telephone in his hand, ready to make a bid. All of a sudden, the auctioneer said "Sold to number 20 on the internet." A couple of minutes later, the phone rang in Art's office and Greg said "I hope that was your bid for three thousand five hundred dollars," which it had been. Art stood up, went to the kitchen for a cup of coffee and since Greg was in Hawaii, I'm not sure what he did but everyone was happy and the Eagles Nest Ranch had a new bull.

Heifer Sale

A heifer sale is a special type of sale when primarily bred heifers are sold to farmers or ranchers to be used as replacements for their herd. Here the buyers are looking for specific breeds that will be added to their already established herds. Eagles Nest Ranch will sell F1 heifers which are a cross-breed of black Angus cows and Hereford bulls which produce black cattle with white faces. There was one time when we had a pen of "black white faced" animals with one calf that was red, because of a recessive red gene in the cow. The bidding began and when the top price was achieved, the auctioneer asked the buyer "Do you want the red one too?" "No, just the black-white faced ones." "Would you take the red one if I lower the price $50?" "No, the buyer responded." "How about if I lower the price $100?" The answer was still "No," so the auctioneer let the black-white faced heifers go out but the red one remained in the ring. The bidding began and all of a sudden, the price was $100.00 above the previous price reached for the others. The bidding went on and a top price was reached. The auctioneer said, "The Rauns will surely fire me" and a good laugh was had by all in the audience.

Killing Time at the Sale Barn

What does a city girl do when waiting patiently for her spouse at a sale barn? She looks through whatever magazines happen to be in front of her on the table in the lobby. They are not the type that one would find in the supermarket with the latest details on the Royal family or who in Hollywood is getting a divorce or having

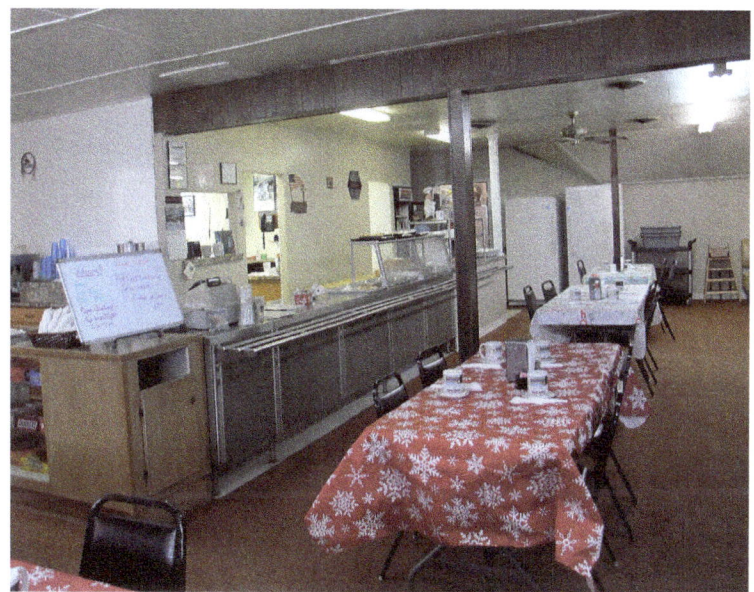

Wonderful home-style food serving sellers and buyers in an absolutely warm and comfortable cafe.

twins. No, these magazines are full of new ideas on raising or protecting animals, new medicines or even new equipment to make ranching easier and more profitable.

While I was doing my share of waiting, I just happened to pick up one such magazine. Looking through it, I saw an item which would work very well on Eagles Nest Ranch. It was a "mineral feeder" which does not sound like much, but minerals, while very expensive, are quite important for the cattle. We had tried various means of distribution but had not found one to be successful. If the mineral, containing calcium and phosphorus, is put in a tub, when rain comes, the mineral gets wet and not favorable for consumption. There have been other ideas promoting tubs on a metal stand with a top over all but the cows and wind seem to destroy it, so once again, not successful.

The one in the magazine, to an untrained eye—which I certainly was, seemed perfect for our situation. Instantly I made note of the telephone number. The feeder was a one piece fiber glass clam-shaped tub with a large opening in the center which would be securely place on the ground in the center of a large semi-truck tire. So far so good! Art did not scoff at the idea of calling the producer and was impressed that the feeder was one which was not only waterproof, but could not be turned over by the cows or wind. We did find out later that it could be upset by bulls rubbing their heads on it but that did not happen often.

One was ordered and proved so successful that more were added. Since purchasing these tubs, the mineral has not been wasted. We have saved more than enough money to pay for more feeders. In this case, there are a variety of minerals such as phosphorus, calcium, potassium, zinc, copper, and cobalt which when mixed together make up the content of the "mineral" bag. When purchasing this item, it is known only as "mineral." (Just another new term in my vocabulary.) The calves also stick their heads in the mineral feeders. They watch their mothers so they follow their lead. What makes it fun to watch is when the calves head come out of the shell, they stick their long tongues out to lick all the crumbs off their faces. It reminds me of a child licking the ice cream on top of the cone!

Unloading our calves, then they wait in the pre-sale pen.

Dog and rider on horse will take animals from yard pens to the sale barn.

Our calves entering the sale ring.

On sale day, parking lot is crowded with trucks and trailers.

JUST ANOTHER DAY

Did you ever have one of those days when it seemed perfect? The day was a beautiful Colorado spring day with bright sun coming in the sewing room window. I was busy sewing a shirt for Greg when the dreaded phone call interrupted the scene. "Can you come to the barn? We need help." So, the sewing project was put aside. I quickly changed my shoes, grabbed a sweatshirt and off to the barn I went.

Greg had been hurt a couple of days prior so Art and I were doing the daily work of feeding the pregnant cows in the east pasture and counting and feeding the cows and calves in the west pasture. He had been severely bruised by a cow pinning him to a gate and constantly butting him on his back side leaving him to limited activity. This was one of those days when every hand was needed as preparations for an upcoming storm were being made.

Thor, the black Hereford bull, needed to be moved to the pasture with the other two bulls. This would not be a problem. For some reason, it seems bulls like to ride in the trailer and this way would be much easier than trying to push him through the pastures. Since bulls, being of the male gender, have a mind of their own, the trailer was loaded, driven to the northwest pasture and unloaded. The three bulls had to fight so one could prove to be the "alpha" bull. Art and I watched as the bulls butted heads, turning each other around in circles, throwing Thor upside down, and finally settling down enough that Art thought everything would be fine. We went back to the barn to check what was next on the list.

Next involved collecting a calf from the east winter pasture that had been born the day before. This time, the Gator was the desired means of transportation. The calf could ride in the back with Art holding him in place. Hopefully, the mom would follow. The calf was found all curled up sound asleep but the mother was nowhere in sight. She had gone to join the other cows in eating which is not unusual when the calf is a day or so old. The calf was successfully loaded in the Gator with Art crunched in beside her and off to the barn we went. OK so far, but which cow eating in the group is the mother?

    The calf was removed and put in an alley way leading into the corral. She started bellowing but no cow came running. Because of this, all the cows in the pasture would have to be lured into the alley and hopefully, one would claim the calf. Treats were poured on the ground. The cows came running but there was one who held back, all the time looking back to where she knew she had left her calf. Finally, she too, joined the group and was put in the alley with the calf. Art and I were hoping we had sorted out the correct cow, but now must just wait to see. The cow walked close to the calf, and after a few turns of sniffing, the cow, sort of thought the calf was hers, but she kept looking back to the pasture. Finally, the calf bellowed and the reunion was complete. But there was a problem! The calf apparently had never nursed as the teats on the cow were so large, the calf could not get hold of one. The cow was then put in a head chute outside the barn and Art went about the task of helping the calf get hooked up. He realized milk was not coming out so he tried milking the cow but to no avail. I was sent to the barn for a cloth and warm water. Maybe that would open the teat. No success! This time I was sent for a fine toothpick that, just maybe, could open the nipple. All the time, Art and the calf were in the chute beside the mom with Art trying to hook the calf up to the mom. For some reason, it seemed as if the cow knew Art was trying to help, so she stood perfectly still. Finally, milk was coming out and, now, Art was holding the calf's mouth to the teat, hoping the calf could nurse. After what seemed to be an eternity, the slurping sound was heard and the calf was nursing. When the calf had finished and wanting to rest, the pair were put in the shed where they could once again bond. Here they would be safe from the storm.

    Back to the barn to check what was next on the list. Feeding! Art got on the tractor and drove to the pasture. While he was rolling out the hay bale, I was counting cows and calves. This does not mean physically counting but each cow is listed on a "check sheet" and when she is seen, her number is marked off. The same procedure is done for the calf. Usually, the calves are close by but there are always a few that are off by themselves. It is not unusual to find one mother surrounded by a number of calves, as if she is baby-sitting so the other mothers can be up eating. On this memorable day, there were four calves in the creek bed, which because of the previous snows, there was standing water. Cows and calves traverse the hills surrounding the creek with the greatest of ease but it is not so easy for humans. I decided the best way to reach the calves was to find a gentle slope for the Gator to navigate. Driving down was easy but thank goodness for the powerful vehicle when returning to the top. The hay had been spread out, cows and calves counted, so back to the barn. All work noted on the sheet had been accomplished. WRONG!

When the ranchers were approaching the barn, I saw a black animal wandering around the parked trailers. "We've got a loose bull," I shouted. The ranchers responded, "What are you talking about?" This black object now came into full view of all of us, Art, Greg and me. "Who is it and how did he get out?" The young bull is still in his corral on the other side of the barn so this was one of the three from the northwest pasture. Once again, "How did he get out?" The solution was simple. He was already by the trailer so Art opened the back door of the trailer while Greg and I pushed him in that direction. Now, as said before, bulls like to ride so once he jumped through the door, it was quickly closed. Art and I got in the truck and once again made the trip north. This time the renegade bull would be put in the northeast pasture where he would be alone.

Back to the barn, park the trailer, hop into the Gator and head to the house. We were thinking the day's project were finished. WRONG AGAIN! Driving up the hill to the house, Art said, "Let's see if we can see the two other bulls through this clearing." None were seen. "Let's drive out further in the pasture where we can see more." "OK" I said as I continued driving further away from the house. "I think I see them over there" said Art directing me to follow his finger pointing down a gully. Yes, they were there, but one was inside the fence where he was supposed to be and the other was on the outside. Art got out of the Gator while I drove ahead to open the nearest closed gate. I then walked back to join Art as he was directing the bull to the now opened gate. This was a success but a mystery remained, "How and where did all three bulls escape from the original location?" This mystery was left to be answered another day because, as predicted, the snow storm was on the horizon. Fixing broken fences would have to wait. One good thing happened from this episode—we were able to have a conversation with our neighbors across the fence.

When finally, back to the house, I looked at my "fit watch" and realized I had six thousand steps recorded with most of them acquired in the answer to the call, "We need help!"

For those wondering—dinner was Chinese carry out!

First Things First!

It was just another one of those days when what we had to do had to be done in a perfect sequence.

It was May and calving was over. The cows/calves were moved to the neighbor's pasture to eat the spring grass found on the "flat top" field on the second of May. However, the grass was not plentiful so the herd had to be moved again. The heifers born prior to last spring would be moved from the corral to a pasture with the bulls so the breeding could begin. The Hereford, Angel and her calf, Cory Thor, would be moved from the pasture to a corral where CT would be weaned. He would then be released into the big world on his own to continue growing and becoming a herd bull. Angel, hopefully, was already pregnant but proof would be determined at a later date.

Where to begin? First, heifers born last spring must vacate the corral, leaving this space open for the gathering of cows and calves returning from the neighbor's pasture. To accomplish this, the procedure was to hopefully get them to walk along the east fence line, of the southeast summer pasture, being persuaded by Art on the Gator with a bag of treats as enticement. This went fairly well after a slight chase on the Gator and a few "Turn around's" called out to the heifers. The total distance from the corral to the north corral is about a mile so the trek was rather slow until the heifers got over the last hill where they could see the corral. All at once, they started running, kicking out their back legs. What a slight to see! Waiting for them on the other side of the fence were the two Hereford bulls, looking forward to some action. This went well! Now on to the next task.

Here there was a slight problem. Not one that would not be solved, but involved a great deal of time and outside help. While the cows and calves were spread out all over the neighbor's pasture, there was one cow, number 0904 who had gotten to the pasture and just couldn't walk any farther. She was not sick; she just would not walk. Her calf was constantly by her side, even though the other calves were having fun running and playing tag in their own little calf way. The cow was old and probably had arthritis in her hip. She was a good mother and had always produced wonderful calves. She could stand, eat and drink water while still allowing her calf to nurse which was a good sign. The vet was called and said there really wasn't anything that could be done for her. WRONG! The ranchers took food and water out to her every day for three days and when it came time to move the other animals from the pasture, Art called in Trey Niemeyer an ex-football player for the

Air Force Academy and who also raises cattle. The plan of attack was to somehow get 0904 into the trailer, take her back to the shed on the ranch where she could be given tender loving care in the form of food, water and protection from bad weather and any possible wild life, such as mountain lions.

The silver trailer would be the best means of transportation because the door is lower to the ground but first of all, the trailer had to be connected to the big Ford 550. While that was happening, I was tying up a stack of feed sacks that had been left in the trailer. This way there would be no distractions for the cow as they can be spooked very easily.

Everything is ready to go. The truck and trailer are driven to the neighbor's pasture, the trailer is backed up as close as it can be to the cow and the hard work begins. A halter was put on the cow. Art was in the trailer, trying to pull 0904 in while Trey was behind pushing. After one unsuccessful try, the cow got her front legs in the trailer and while Trey was pushing, Art, with the aid of a "come along" winch, pulled her in. Door closed, cow standing, off went truck and trailer to the shed. It was a successful trip! When in the shed, 0904 got out of the trailer and immediately laid down. Water and hay were put by in close proximity so she could reach it. Only problem—where was her calf? It was still out in the pasture. Quite possibly the mother had said, "Why don't you go and play with your friends? I will be all right here."

The next phase of the moving operation was to gather all the cows/calves in the corral before releasing them into the southwest summer pasture. We rode back out to the pasture in the Gator. Art was driving the Gator and once the cows started moving toward the corral, he would drive ahead dropping treats as he drove back through the gate to the home pasture. The cows/calves followed faithfully. I was walking behind the herd, bring up any stragglers, of which there were three little calves. Every now and then, they would stop, looking back to where they had been, but then would take off running to catch up with the others. There was one calf who was stopping more often. It would stand perfectly still, and continue to look back. I suddenly realized it was 2104 whose mother had been taken to the shed. With encouragement I kept saying, "Keep going, your mother is in the shed." Fortunately, the calf kept going.

When the group got close to the corral within sight of 0904, she let out a very loud "Moo!" By this time, with the frantic waving of my hands, Art had opened the gate to the corral where 0904 was waiting. Her calf stopped in her tracks, "mooed" and took off running through the gate leading to the shed and was quickly united with her mom. "Well, that went well!

The moving continued as gates were opened to the southwest summer pasture." The cows/calves moved very fast as they realized there was a lot of green grass waiting for them. At this point, I went to the house to get ready to attend a graduation party. But Not So Quick!!! The phone rang, the neighbor was calling, "Did you mean to leave these other cows and calves on the hill?" "Oh, my gosh" was the response, "No, I'll be right there." Putting shoes on as I ran to the car, the Excursion was now put into service to help in this roundup. No more walking for I had already had my exercise for the day. Once again, Art drove the Gator to the top of the hill where he got behind the small group and started yelling, "GO!." Success was achieved. This small herd came down the hill to where I was waiting, guiding the animals to the open gate into the home pasture. Once again, the cows did what they were told to do—as if they understood every word and the mission was accomplished.

Not to leave the readers wondering what happened to cow 0904 and her calf, fast forward one week. As Art was putting grain in the tub for her, she gave him a bit of a welcome by butting him on his hind side. She was up, anxious for her feed and was walking to the tank for water. The calf had been nursing so it was a perfect ending. Oh yes, the calf has been by the mother's side all week long and was being fed a starter supplement after "go for" had gone to the feed store for this special feed. The cows/calves are enjoying the green grass which is growing now since the ranch has received some very valuable moisture. The cow 0904 is doing so well, she will be turned out to a grassy area and water close by so she may continue to improve.

"First things first" does not always hold true, especially when the door of opportunity opens and action needs to be taken. In between the time of getting the lame cow and her calf reunited, Art noticed Angel and Cory Thor by the southeast fence line. This was good because since they were already going to be moved, this meant they were physically closer to their destination. "Let's go ahead and bring them in now" was the thinking. Problem was, there was a baby calf on the other side of the fence and Angel must have thought she needed to be a baby sitter as the calf's mother was away out eating grass. I got Angel and Cory started up the fence line but all of a sudden, Angel stopped, possibly looking to see if the calf was following. "Oh, please don't go back," was my thinking but suddenly, Angel saw the other cow running toward her calf. What a relief that was for me as the procession continued onward to the designated corral. What a day it was! "All's well that ends well!" and all the "firsts" were accomplished.

On our ranch the rule is, the CATTLE come first! The cattle are fed before we eat and are bedded down before we go to bed. They are our number one priority. If a storm approaches, they are secured first and finally we take shelter. Cattle ranching, even on a small ranch, is not a part time job. Situations arise that require IMMEDIATE attention. Immediate means "right now" whatever you are doing at the time! There is no "in a little bit." There is no "Why not later." This is one time the "Why Not?" does not mean later, it means NOW!

That isn't really the end of the story. We got cleaned up, dressed in party clothes and went to the graduation party two hours late. This was okay as we got individual attention and were as reunited with old friends.

For those of you wondering what happened to the sick cow and her calf, the answer is unfortunately the cow passed away after a few weeks. Fortunately, her calf who had learned to eat Purina Calf Starter during her mom's decline was adopted by Angel, a black Hereford cow, and her much older weaned calf Cory. The calf became known as Little Bit. Cory became a wonderful big brother. It was fun to watch Cory and Little Bit grazing in the pasture. They stuck together like glue. They were both fed dry feed since Angel was no longer giving milk. They shared Purina feed in the same feed bunk. Little Bit will be a wonderful and beautiful heifer that will ultimately serve as a mother cow in someone's commercial herd.

TALES ABOUT TAILS

The following tales are not necessarily about tails but are about the creatures to which the tails are attached.

Stuck Golf Cart and the John Deere Gator

The first tale of many occurred early in our ranching days, Art had gone out in the golf cart to check on the cows in the pasture; it was snowing and when driving on a slope, the cart slid into a water hole and got stuck. He walked back to the barn and told me the red truck was needed along with a driver and be sure to bring a rope tow which was needed to get the cart out of the swamp. Equipment in hand, we took off heading to the pasture. The cows knew when the red truck went to the pasture that food would be imminent. However, this time as they followed the truck and watched it go down into the gully, they must have realized it was not for feeding but for some other purpose. The cows stood side by side on the ledge of the hill watching as the truck and me as the driver went about pulling the cart out of the water. They started mooing as if to say, "Hey, girls, come see what this idiot rancher has done this time." When all was accomplished, the cows went back to their eating of hay. No cubes this time! The cows were probably thinking, "if only he had been watching us, he would have known it was wet down there and should not drive anything, especially that golf cart down into the gully!"

The rough riding golf cart, although always dependable and used for many years, was replaced by a much safer and comfortable vehicle, a John Deere Gator (TM). The cart was taken from the ranch, once again on a flatbed truck, to a Golf Cart dealer

Curious calves crowding around grandchildren, Katie and Michael as they were doing the daily headcount.

who liked the challenge of repairing a dinosaur. He seemed extremely pleased with his purchase. We were happy for him and even happier that the cart would not be placed on the ranch junk pile. Of course, the grandchildren were sorry to see it go as they spent many hours bouncing around the ranch on it. I was especially glad to see it replaced as I had on more than a few occasions gotten high centered on rocks in the pasture. That happened one time when I was alone on the ranch. I had to call on neighbors to help push the cart off so I could continue my mission of checking cows and calves in the pasture. It was impossible for me to push it and steer at the same time, but as a woman, it took courage for me to call someone for help!

The first Gator was replaced by larger, more powerful one, with wider tires, providing a much smoother ride. It easily traverses the uneven terrain. Its bench seat can hold the driver and two other relatively small people. Others could possibly ride in the box on the back, but it would not be at all that comfortable. One day there were two young men visiting the ranch and while one fellow sat originally on the seat, it wasn't long when both were standing up in the box, stating they could "see everything better." All I could say was, "Hang On!" The box is great for hauling mineral and feed out to the cows and calves so in reality it is used for something every day. Lights and seat belts are standard and the only thing missing is a horn that we could use when rounding up the cattle. But our cattle are so well trained (spoiled) that when they see the Gator, they are quite sure they will be given treats.

What's All That Racket?

Have you ever seen cows react to sirens? Out here in the country, sirens are not common so it was amusing to watch the reaction of the cows when the rescue units went past on the road. The sirens could be heard coming from quite a distance away. When the noise got closer, the animals ran to the fence. They stood in a line, side by side, heads over the fence, waiting to see what was causing that horrible noise. The fire truck came first and the cows just remained standing there and then the rescue unit came by. This time, the cows turned and, almost in a stampede fashion, took off running away from the fence. They came, they saw, and do not want to hear or see those noisy vehicles again!

Lost Babies

One day as we were cleaning out the barn, getting it ready for more birthing action, a cow came to the barn door and bellowed loudly three or four times. She then turned and walked away. Art and I continued with our cleaning until the cow came back and bellowed again. This time, I said, "I think she has lost her calf and can't find it." When the cows and calves are put out in the pasture, the cows will take their calves away from the group for a couple of days so the bonding process may begin. After the second day, the cow will come up, joining the herd to eat, then return to her calf at some remote place. In this case, the momma forgot where she had left her baby and was asking us to help her find it. Off we went on foot looking in all possible places. The cow stayed back in the field, carefully watching where we were going. We found the calf sound asleep on a faraway hill. We got him up, thinking we could walk him back to his mother, but no, he turned around and went right back to where he had been, exactly where the momma had told him to stay. We called to the mamma to come and she came running. The interesting part of this is that there were other mothers in the pasture but only this one came running. She got next to the calf's ear and bellowed loudly three times as if to say, "Don't you ever do that again. I have been worried sick about you." After that, the two were always together.

Teenagers

Once when the calves were what might be considered "teenagers," there was a cow bellowing in the pasture close to the house. I was busy in the house but the noise did arouse suspicion, so I went to see who it was. The cow was OK but probably needed her calf to nurse. I thought the cow and calf would eventually pair up so went back to the house. When the noise did not stop, I went back out, this time to find the calf, which I did. The calf was on the other side of the drive, sound asleep, but within hearing distance. Being a "teenager," the calf apparently did not want to be interrupted at that particular moment. When I called "Hey, Mamma" the cow came running and the calf finally woke up. He realized his mother was close by, so he must have decided he was hungry as he got up and started nursing. Relief for the cow!

Cow Paths

Have you ever heard "that road is nothing more than a cow path?" Probably not in this era but back in the "dark ages" when there were no super highways, there were some country roads that would fall into the category as a "cow path." Why do cows make paths? The path is always the easiest and usually the shortest route to water. With each rotation from pasture to pasture during the summer months, a new path is produced. Once again, this is not proven scientifically but can be proven by watching the cows. The other thing is, that a path left from the year before is never used. The second path will probably be quite close to the first one and will eventually wear the ground down becoming sort of a ditch of about two inches deep and ten or more inches wide. The other observation is that when cows are walking to water, they quite often are in a line, with calves running alongside. If the cow has lost sight of her youngster, she will stop, look around, step out of line and wait for the calf to catch up. If not successful, the cow will start mooing and will stay in one spot until the calf joins the procession. When herding cows, they will move easier if the lead cow is on the path. But, it's not always easy for us to find that particular cow! Humans also find the paths more inviting than walking through the grass and rocks found in the pastures.

There was one time early in the ranching days when I was sent out to the pasture to bring the cows into the barn. It was time for some routine procedure such as inserting a fly tag. Working them in the barn chutes was part of the program. I was on the golf cart and had gotten the cows successfully out of one pasture. When the cows were in the second pasture, about half way to the barn, they quickly ran past me and right to the barn. Greg was waiting for them and was rather upset thinking his mom had made the cows run. When I got to the barn, he said, "Don't make them run." My answer was, "I didn't! They just passed me up like I was standing still. They are ready for their treats." Don't ever think cows aren't smart!

I Can See Him From Here!

Art had been in the pasture doing the daily checking of cows and new calves. He had found all the cows but one calf was missing. The mother was eating with the others and did not seem upset or bellowing. Neither of us will give up looking until all cows and calves are found and marked off the list, especially after a storm

A well-worn cow path is usually the shortest route to water.

or snow as had happened this time. I arrived on the scene as Art was coming into the barn saying there was one calf missing. We both took off in the Gator, covering what we thought was every inch of the pasture. But to no avail. We went back to where the mother was and watched her, thinking she might take off to find the calf herself. No such luck. Finally, I said to the cow, "Momma, where is your baby?" I repeated this a second time, after which the cow, turned and walked back to where the other cows and calves were eating. She sniffed a couple of calves, then turned, facing west, just standing there and looking out into the pasture. We decided we would head off in that direction, hoping the cow would follow. No, she just stood still but continued looking, always in the same direction. Once again, we went out to the pasture, this time searching every nook and cranny, under ever tree root, which is a favorite spot to hide calves and still no baby. Heading back to the barn we wondered where in the world could that calf be. All of a sudden we noticed the cow had been joined by two other cows, all looking in the same direction. Art realized there were two calves laying in sort of a gully, so we looked there again. I said, "Is that a white face over there?" The lost calf was only a few feet from the other two calves and somehow had been missed on all the other searches. This was not the first time such an incident has occurred and maybe it is just my imagination but I really believe cows can communicate and understand what humans say to them. If dogs can be trained and understand orders from humans, why can't it apply also to cows?

Cows As Socialites

A cow is not just a cow but an animal that is also a very social creature. There are cows on Eagles Nest Ranch that like to have their noses rubbed or being rubbed under their chin as do most dogs and cats. There has been one observation (although not proven scientifically) that if a cow has been in a group for a period of time and is removed, she will find her way back to that original group.

One such incident occurred when there had been a group of five late birthing cows who had been together in the pasture for a long period of time. When one finally delivered her calf, she and her calf were put out with the large group of cows in the larger pasture. But what happened was, the next day or so, she was found standing by the fence with her calf by her side, waiting to be put back in her most familiar pasture with her previous group of cows. When this group of five were finally turned out with the larger group, these five would always be seen together.

There was another time when a cow who did not have a calf was turned out to the larger pasture which she apparently did not like, so she jumped over the fence to be back with her friends. This is hard to explain, but it has happened more than once. Just a part of nature that cannot be explained by humans. Apparently, cows do not like to just gossip over the fences but prefer face to face cow visits.

We were told the story about a cow that we had sold to a farm in Nebraska where the farmer was out in his pasture one dark night when he felt a nudge at his elbow. He turned and was face to face with the black animal who had been a pet here at the ranch and who liked to have her head rubbed. He said he performed as the cow had hoped and as a result, continued being his pet. Looking back through our records, Art realized this cow was Norma, one of the few calves that had acquired a name. She had also been a bottle baby so had received extra attention.

CALF STORIES

Every Day Is Full Of New Experiences

One day we had driven out to the larger pasture to do our daily check on the cows and calves. When the calves get older, we will check every other day. If there had been a thunderstorm or some other unusual weather we checked again, making sure every animal was OK. This particular day, we had taken a plastic bag with us so we could pick any trash that might have blown in as a result of high winds. Both of us had walked away from the cart in opposite directions and neither of us were watching the golf car. But there was one nosey calf that went to investigate the dark object left in the cart. Like any baby, the first thing he did was to put the found plastic bag in his mouth. When we tried to retrieve it, the calf started running. The faster he ran, the more air got in the bag and then a funny noise sounded as the bag was hitting his body. The noise startled the cows who then began running after the calf. What a circus that was! This continued for a few minutes until Art was finally able to grab hold of the bag. This stopped the noise and the cows walked away, going back to their grazing. The calves are so nosey, they have even pulled the keys from the ignition so we are now very careful to take the keys whenever we leave the cart.

No Sleep Tonight

Our early home in the barn is now used when we need to be close to pregnant cows and new mothers. All other times we retreat to our real home situated on the hill 200 feet higher and out of sight of the barn. In June when the cows/calves are moved to the larger summer pasture, there are nights when we get little sleep. We live in our house when birthing is over and have the windows open, enjoying the fresh Colorado air. Here begins the problem. When the cows are moved, they immediately explore all of the new pasture searching for grass but many calves still take naps and sleep soundly, stretched out, enjoying the heat from the sun and do not follow their moms. So, all night, or so it seems, the cows are bellowing for their young. It is not unusual to hear the calf answering and this back-and-forth noise continues until they finally get paired up and the calf gets its stomach filled. Of course, there are times when I think Art should get out of bed to check on the noise but he responds, "The animals are just fine" and turns over and goes back to sleep. Once a mother, always a mother!

Let's Play Tag

It was a beautiful Colorado blue sky day without a cloud in the sky. The cows were grazing on fresh green grass while the calves were stretched out enjoying the sun. They were so sound asleep; a person could walk right up to them and they would not move. I was in the barn looking out my "window on the world" watching the pregnant cows in the corral and hoping one would give birth soon. Out of the corner of my eye I saw motion in the west winter pasture. There were three cows and their calves in the pasture closest to the barn when all of a sudden, one of the calves had gotten up. He stretched out with his front legs way out as if saying "I am so big." His back legs were also stretched out. When he got his body all back together, he gave a little wiggle becoming fully awake. He was ready for some action! Looking around, the other calves were sleeping and the mothers were busy eating. What to do? All of a sudden, he took off running toward one of the sleeping calves. He nudged the calf with his nose but nothing happened. Off he went to the third calf doing the same routine. This time he got a response. The third try was a success as this calf got up, stretched and took off running, chasing the instigator. By now, the second calf was up, wide awake and apparently not wanting to be left out of the fun. All three calves were running and chasing each other as fast as they could. Their tails were sticking straight out, sort of like horses in a race. One calf would run up to another one with his nose serving as a hand as he tagged the other calf, then this calf would take off, trying to tag the other one. (Just like little boys playing tag on the school playground.) Sometimes, after running so fast, it was hard for them to stop. It looked as if their rear was coming around to their front, sort of like a truck trying to stop with a trailer on behind that slides to the side, (really hard to describe but fun to watch.) When the game was over and the mothers were ready to join the herd, all three cows and calves paired up and moved to where they might spend the night. Calves can out run their mothers and when they get too far ahead, they will stop and wait for mom to catch up. After all she is the one that provides the food and for a growing calf, that is the number one concern!

I'm Not Lost But Where is Mom?

It is not unusual for a calf to be misplaced but this time it was the mom. If a child is lost in a department store or such, there would be an announcement over the loud speaker saying, "Would the lost mom of Johnny please come to the front desk." But no such announcement was made and the calf was the one left searching. This calf was probably about six weeks old and was smaller than the other calves born in the spring. The cows and calves had been grazing in a large pasture and all except about six cows and calves had gone to the corral for water. The calf went along, thinking her mother was in the group. WRONG! This poor little calf checked out all the cows but none would claim her. So, leaving the corral, she went back out to the pasture. But not knowing exactly where to look, she just stood there looking back to where she had been. All of a sudden, she saw two cows coming along the fence line. The calf ran toward them but the cows pushed her away. Her mother was not one of them. Back to watching. "Oh, what is that coming over the hill? Could it be? Would it be?" The calf let out a high pitched "Moo" and the cow answered. Joy, beyond joy. The lost mom had been found. The calf ran to meet her and when together, the calf immediately started nursing. When the stomach was full, the calf laid down right on the spot and went sound asleep. The mother stayed close by grazing the grass. Water for her had to wait until the calf woke up and they would go to the corral together.

Can Cows and Humans Communicate?

Yes, they can! After carefully observing the cows, I think if I could read their minds, I might even be able to forecast the weather. Now I am wondering if cows really understand humans when we speak to them. This idea has never been proven but to me, it does seem very plausible.

I have never seen a cow's brain so I have no idea as to the size of one. I feel cows are very smart and if humans' souls "stop, look and listen" we might even learn a thing or two from our four-legged friends.

Our cows are very docile so when we hear a loud "Moo" we immediately take notice. I believe in such an incident, the cow is trying to tell us something, especially if the "Mooing" continues.

The cows know our voices which is evident when we move them from one pasture to another. I believe they understand "Go" or "Turn Around." I am not sure if they actually know the words or is it just the inflection of our voices. They also know us by our clothes which might explain how closely they watch us. If we go into the west winter pasture where the new moms and calves are, wearing different coats, the cows will take their babies and walk away from us. This also happens when we have visitors with us. Once we say something such as "It's OK. We're just showing off your babies." Then the cows will stop, apparently realizing they are safe, and will eventually come to us for cubes.

When Art goes to the pasture he shouts, "Su Boss!" Possibly a Danish word learned from his father when he would be calling the cows. The cows will raise their heads, even from a long distance and look toward Art. Possibly they are thinking, "What is he trying to tell us?" They do seem to know when they hear him that something is about to happen and especially if he opens a gate. Cows cannot pass up an open gate!

"ON THE ROAD AGAIN"

Early on in the operation of Eagles Nest Ranch, we realized that grazing on corn stalks in Nebraska would be cheaper and a most convenient way to winter cows. To feed the cows on the ranch during the winter meant hauling hay from wherever it could be purchased. There were years of drought which meant hay crops were high in demand and hard to find. Art had family in Nebraska who raised corn and were very willing to let our cows graze their corn stalks.

The leaves left on a corn stalk as well as corn and even corn cobs left on the ground after harvest serves as a great food for cows. This is not an unusual idea as it is a very common practice throughout the Midwest. One hundred sixty acres will provide enough feed for sixty cows for three months which was exactly the number and time needed for "winter camp." The chosen field had a battery powered electric wire strung around the perimeter, a large water tank was positioned and water was delivered timely by truck.

Everything was ready, so the trucking began. At first the "good old red truck" pulling a twenty-foot trailer filled with nine to ten 1,000-pound cows made the trip to Art's sister's farm located south of Minden. The first year when there were only thirty-seven first calf heifers to transport this was done in four round trips covering a total of 712 miles and six hours each way. The cows were delivered during the middle of November, depending on weather, returning to the Colorado ranch the middle of February, in time for the start of calving. This operation gave Art an excuse to stop for coffee, either at his sister's, brother's or his mother's home in Minden. The best part of all of this was that Art's 96-year-old mother was very interested in the operation and she was able to see the cows during their "winter camp" in Nebraska.

We are thankful for the trailer salesman who gave us the name of the Ford dealer in Ardmore, Oklahoma where the best price was always available. The first truck purchased there was a F350 in 1996. We flew to Oklahoma City where the truck, having been described over the phone, was picked up. We put the first miles on that truck by visiting family in Stillwater and friends in LeFlore before driving back to Colorado. What a wonderful way to break in a truck seeing scenery and places never before observed.

In 2001 due to an increase in cow numbers, a Ford 550 flatbed truck was purchased to be driven by Art. Behind it now was a thirty-foot aluminum trailer able to carry twelve 1,300-pound cows comfortably for the six-hour ride. The "good old red truck" would continue pulling the twenty-foot trailer with eight cows with me as the driver. Our theme song was "On The Road Again" as we went merrily on our way.

The "good old red truck" was "put out to pasture" in 2005, replaced by a white Ford 350. It was still a stick shift operation but by now I knew how to down shift and how to keep the truck in the center of my lane. I was much more confident driving now but I had to add a thick seat cushion for comfort. The cows were now being taken to our farm in Loup City, Nebraska about 65 miles north of Minden. The trucking route changed due to the new location but provided great new scenery.

The purpose of this section is to help the readers picture what we were seeing as the cattle trips were made from Elbert, Colorado, to Minden and Loup City, Nebraska. Hopefully, it will help in understanding the "trucking stories" later in this chapter.

Route to Minden

Even though we have made many cattle trips to Minden, it was never boring. The scenery, although the same, is always different. For those thinking eastern Colorado, western Kansas and middle Nebraska is nothing but flat land, Art says "There is a lot to see, if you are really looking."

When driving to Minden, the first seven and a half miles are the same starting point as the trip to Loup City except instead of turning north, we continue east on Colorado 86. Here the two-lane highway goes up and down high hills, some high enough that I had to learn how to down shift the F350 to maintain my speed. Then I had to slow down to go around the many curves. This highway is known to be the shortest route from I-70 to Denver and if driving west, it is a beautiful drive with the whole Rocky Mountains front range in full view. Highway C86 ends at I-70 west of Limon. There are towns along I-70 but the largest is Burlington where there is a nice welcome center and a museum depicting early Colorado history. After driving east for twelve miles, one may read the sign "You are now leaving Colorado" and soon, the sign for Kanorado appears. Needing a coffee break can be accomplished at the Kansas Welcome Center, nine miles from the state line. Gas is always cheaper in Kansas so coffee or not, the fuel tank will be filled in Goodland.

Staying on I-70 to the east edge of Colby, a left turn off I-70 is made and going a few miles before making a right-hand turn onto U.S. 24. Taking this route, the city of Colby is bypassed and missing the local stop and start driving is much easier on the driver's nerves. U.S. 24 is a two-lane road, passing many irrigated corn fields and in spring, green fields of the growing winter wheat. From here we will take off at an angle on U.S. 83 and then onto U.S. 383.

This route goes through many small towns with main streets away from the highway. There is one town that has its school and athletic field close enough to the highway that a "School Zone - Reduce Speed" sign is posted for all to see and obey. Mostly on the west side of the road will be grain elevators close to railroad tracks holding hopper cars waiting to be filled after harvest. Also, along this track will be seen long lengths of old box cars that have been there for many years. They are covered with all sorts of art work which quite probably would never make it into an art show of any kind. Once in a while a work crew might been seen but very seldom is a working freight train seen on the track. In the spring, farmers are busy working their fields, the winter wheat is growing and irrigation systems may be working depending on rain or no rain. In the fall, farmers are harvesting crops, hauling grain to the elevators and leaving large piles of beautifully mixed colored milo or corn on the ground because the elevators are filled to capacity. These piles may also be seen by cattle feed lots along the route where they may or may not be covered. Most generally these piles are covered with white plastic held in place by numerous heavy tires.

An interesting site on the horizon is the twin spires of the Leoville Catholic Church seen shortly after passing through Selden. There is one spot, a farm silo west of Norton, Kansas that Art has designated the "100-mile marker." In driving to Minden, he knows he has exactly 100 miles to go. In reverse, he has driven one hundred miles and still has 256 more to go before reaching the home ranch. Then onward onto U.S. 383 where Prairie Dog Creek is crossed many times. I always wondered why anyone would name a creek after prairie dogs since they are considered a pest by ranchers, but they didn't ask me. Reading in *Roadside Kansas*, I found out that the black tailed prairie dog is quite common in this area and by burrowing the land, they may improve the soil. So, while not being a favorite animal, they can be tolerated but that in itself is debatable. It remains questionable why they ever named both a creek and Prairie Dog State Park on U.S. 36 after them. This Park has been passed many times as the we continue on U.S. 383, joining U.S. 36 for a few miles before arriving in Norton, Kansas.

U.S. 36 claims to be the shortest route to Indianapolis from Denver and while it is a beautiful route if one is going to Indy in a car, it is not so good when hauling cattle. There are many hills and many, many slow traffic areas due to the number of small towns along the way. We continue north through Norton and if fuel was not purchased in Goodland, Norton is the next best place. Leaving Norton, is the Kansas Correction Center with notices on the highway, "Do Not Pick Up Hitchhikers."

Shortly after entering Nebraska is the Harlan County Reservoir. It was construction in 1952 by the U.S. Corp of Engineers and covers 13,250 acres. It was formed by damming the Republican River, which starts in eastern Colorado south of I-70 between mile markers 371 and 383 and ends in Phillips County, Kansas, close to the Nebraska and Kansas county line. The Republican River valley has quite a history dating back to the 1850s when the Nebraska Territory was being formed. In 1872, Republican City was established, unfortunately, not a wise move as the Native Americans had told the early settlers not to build close to the river. On May 31, 1935, twenty-four inches of rain caused a flood which wiped out the city "within minutes." This was the same storm as the May 31st flood causing storm in Elbert County. Republican City was rebuilt in 1952 on higher ground, two miles north of the original site where, even now, foundations of original buildings are visible when the water level is low.

Crossing the reservoir is always interesting to see what the water level is and what water foul are enjoying the lake. It is also a great place for fishing; however, the water level is always changing. The first town after the reservoir is Alma. The highway once again misses the town but there are businesses, restaurants, service stations, and more on the highway that cater to motorists. Before getting to the next town of Holdrege many beautifully well-kept farmsteads are seen. Cattle are seen in the rolling pastures and are getting water from the ponds in the valleys. Between Holdrege and Minden are fields of the usual crops of milo, corn, soybeans, alfalfa hay and wheat. Here also seen is a busy, working train track. It has hopper cars parked by the elevators and black tank cars waiting by the Ethanol plant as Ethanol is a by-product of corn. In the middle of the night, the Amtrak from Chicago to California uses this track. I have never seen these trains on the track but I have heard whistles many times at 2 A.M. as go they through Minden.

Minden, Nebraska is called the "Christmas City" because in 1936 lights were strung from the top of the Kearney County Court House radiating out to the surrounding streets. The lights, lighting the area from Thanksgiving through New Year's Day, may be seen from many miles away. This tradition also includes a Christmas pageant performed by local talent and choirs. There are many other community activities prior to Christmas such as the decorating of trees by the Women's Garden Club.

Probably the most beautiful building in Minden is the Opera House, constructed in the fall of 1891 and finished in the spring of 1892. After closing in the 1940s, it was occupied by a variety of businesses. In 1999-2000, it was completely refurbished to its original beauty. On the first floor is a welcoming center, an art gallery and large meeting hall suited for all types of functions. Going from the first floor to the second floor is a beautiful wood staircase, although not a circular one, it has a landing before the stairs continue upward. On the second floor is an auditorium and stage for various types of entertainment, and absolutely the most beautiful ceiling ever produced. An artist from California toured Kearney County getting ideas from which he produced the four rural seasons including various important historical places in the county. During performances on stage when the lights are turned off, the audience is privilege to view a night time sky including shooting stars. The art work, the lighting system with the stars is absolutely spectacular.

No, I am not associated with the Minden Chamber of Commerce but I was so enamored with the beauty of this building, I want to share it with everyone. Tours are available and if one is interested in history and old buildings, this is truly one to visit.

Minden is also the home of Pioneer Village where there are many signs along the highways advertising it. A tour through the museum is worth the time as for some, it brings back memories, for others, such as grandparents traveling with grandchildren, it is a time of sharing life without electricity and television.

I am not a tour guide nor do I work for the Tourist Bureaus of Colorado, Kansas or Nebraska. Had I not taken up ranching in Colorado, I would still be believing that Kansas and Nebraska are nothing but flat open spaces. Making the many trips transporting cattle I have observed so much of God's beauty. It was a case of being at the right place at the right time. In the spring, Sand Hill Crane migrate north and feed in the many farm fields surrounding the Platte River. Crossing the Harlan

County Dam, I saw egrets along with a variety of ducks. In the fall the sky was filled with the beautiful white snow geese migrating south. Also, all during the year, bald eagles are seen in the trees along the Platte. I will never forget seeing the hen pheasant crossing the highway with her six chicks, stopping traffic as they crossed the highway or the pelican flying overhead in Nebraska. Of course, it was always enjoyable watching the sun rise as the we headed east and the spectacular sunsets seen driving west through Kansas and eastern Colorado as the Crepuscular rays were radiating though gaps in the clouds. What a breathtaking experience!

Route to Loup City

When traveling with children/grandchildren, we were always playing games such as "I spy" or "I see something green or whatever color." There was also the game of spotting a letter to complete the alphabet. Now instead of playing games, we "connect the dots" or "which dot represents which significant mile marker."

We have traveled the route from Elbert to the farm in Minden, Nebraska many times but have gone to the farm in Loup City even more. The trip to Minden is always the same route, however the one to Loup City may be altered a bit. The trip is always made in good weather with a few exceptions being made when weather changes while the truckers are in route.

The trip to Loup City begins driving through Kiowa, the county seat of Elbert, turning north on the Kiowa Bennett Road, continuing through Bennett, passing the school and a beautiful cemetery on the outskirts of town. Continuing north to where tall elevators are seen on the skyline. These are the main features of Roggen where we will get on Interstate 76. After driving for seventy-two miles, it is time to break out the homemade breakfast sandwiches and a cup of coffee. On the north side of this highway is a huge dairy farm in Wiggins. Here are seen Holstein cows which produce milk for Colorado residents. There are stacks and stacks of round hay bales, large pit silos filled with corn and a number of little A-frame fiberglass huts which are homes for individual new born dairy calves. Going a bit further, we cross over were the Kiowa Creek flows north to join the South Platte River.

Fort Morgan is exactly 100 miles from Eagles Nest Ranch. Here is where sugar beets are processed with a sign "GW Sugar" on one of the buildings. In the fall, trucks filled with sugar beets are observed coming from all directions. Twelve miles further is a quick stop at McDonalds at Brush. This is only if I did not make my famous "breakfast sandwiches."

Thirty-three miles eastward is Sterling, where if one gets off the interstate and drives through the town, there is a park where old trees have been carved to depict living creatures. North of the interstate and east of Sterling, rising on the horizon, is a wind farm which may be seen for many miles. Of course, the position of the sun helps in the sighting the many towers. There are many small towns dotting the landscape but most are at a distance from the main highway. This area of the state is definitely agricultural. The South Platte River which parallels I-76 supplies the water for the irrigation of crops, especially corn, and where there is corn, there is also cattle. There are also rolling hills covered with native grass on which the cattle love to graze.

Forty-five miles onward to Julesburg, a noted pioneer town in the early settlement days of Colorado. The town itself is not on I-76 but is closer to Interstate 80. Five miles east the two Interstates merge, I-76 ends and the heavily traveled Interstate 80 becomes the main east-west highway.

A fuel stop will always be made in Big Springs, Nebraska. Here is a small but very friendly truck stop. The people are pleasing, the available food is great and the rest rooms (most important) are clean. The terrain along Interstate 80 is flat because it follows along the South Platte River. To the north are hills, commonly known as the "sand hills."

After four hours and fifteen minutes of driving we arrive in Ogallala, Nebraska which is where we sell our cattle. We have become friends with the people at the sale barn, at the Quality Inn and REAL friends with the local Ford dealer, as later explained.

From Ogallala, driving only nineteen miles, we find Paxton, home of the famous "Ole's Big Game" Restaurant. This was an important stop for Art one time as he had truck trouble on a Sunday afternoon. It required the attention of a blacksmith, located by the waiter at Ole's, the blacksmith left a graduation party to help the driver in despair. Only in *small* towns is this help willingly given. Driver, truck and trailer were back on the road in an hour and a half with a better than new trailer hitch.

Now on U.S. 30 driving thirteen miles eastward is Sutherland, home of a large Ethanol plant where ethanol is produced from corn. The plant always has a line of black tank rail cars waiting to be filled for transporting. Six miles further is Hershey, but no chocolate factories there.

This region of Nebraska is relatively flat. The highways and rail systems were positioned in what is considered the river valley. To the north are the "sand hills" formed from sediment blown in from river beds east of the Rocky Mountains fifteen thousand years ago. In the spring on the thirteen miles between Hershey and North Platte will be seen thousands of migrating Sand Hill Crane. North Platte is also the site of the largest rail yard in the world. North Platte residents and those of surrounding towns were famous for supplying sandwiches, fruit, cakes/cookies to every troop train traveling on the Union Pacific line during World War II from 1941 to 1946, not missing a single train.

At North Platte where the North and South Platte rivers merge, the route changes from US 30 to US 83 going northeast for twenty-five miles to Nebraska 92. After sixteen miles, this journey goes through an area of rolling hills and deep valleys covered with a variety of trees. If there when the sun is hitting the rolling hills, the scenery is absolutely spectacular. The hills are mostly grazing areas but there are valley fields covered with corn. Unfortunately, one time the fields had been hit with a terrible hail storm and the stocks of corn were stripped bare. All anyone could say was, Oh, Oh, Oh! It was such a disaster and not a beautiful site.

This route continues through the little town of Arnold whose main street is off the highway and has never been visited by either one of us. There is, however, a farm supply store on the highway which was the source of the mineral feeder that I saw advertised in a magazine at a cattle sale.

After driving for twenty-four miles, we are at Merna where if one would be traveling west on N 2, they would be taken through the heart of the sand hills. Continuing east the road runs parallel with the Burlington Northern Santa Fe railroad with its one hundred and ten coal cars and two or three diesel engine trains hauling coal out of Wyoming. From Merna going east jointly on N 2 and N 92 for twenty-three miles it is not unusual to see three to six coal trains along this road. Supposedly, there is a new train every fifteen minutes—but I never timed the trains. There was one day when I was driving by myself, listening to the radio and carefully watching the road when all of a sudden, a train beside me blew its whistle and I nearly about jumped out of my skin. After that I paid special attention to the track even if there were no trains in sight!

Continuing on eastward, the highway drops into a valley and the city of Broken Bow. The son of the town founder, Wilson Hewitt, found a broken Pawnee bow on the banks of a nearby creek. After the town was named "Broken Bow" pieces of the bow were broken and given away as souvenirs. The only piece left is on display at the Custer County Museum. How about that for some history? A beautiful golf course greets us before we enter the town center. Here the Custer County Court House is located in a square block surrounded by various businesses. We have spent many nights there in a local motel. It was not a quiet place as the motel is only about fifty yards from the rail tracks. The whistles of the train begin at one edge of town and continue through to the other edge of town. At one time, a train derailed going through town causing a change in the traffic pattern for a while. This made an interesting tale to tell. I am sure the locals enjoyed the peace and quiet while the track was closed for a spell.

Leaving Broken Bow, we will turn off the joint highway at Ansley to continue east on N 92. Up and down high hills, passing beautiful old farmsteads, trees on either side of the roads which were planted during the drought years,1929-1935, to serve as wind breaks. The road continues down into the Middle Loup River valley into Loup City. As seen quite often in other locations, the Sherman County Court House is located in a square block, surrounded by businesses. There is the Frederick Hotel and Café, built in 1913 and recently refurbished. There is a hardware store, grocery store, a snack shop, and of course, a bank surrounding the square. The Colony motel is located on the highway and its busiest time is the fall hunting season. As we pass the Colony we know there is only six miles to go before reaching the farm. Off the highway, onto mud roads, especially after rain or snow, a left-hand turn is made. To the top of the hill and a right-hand turn, the farm's driveway is in sight. After 406 miles and seven hours of riding, the cows are going to be released from the trailer. They immediately remember where they are and know exactly how to locate water, grass and corn in the field. FREE AT LAST! The occupants of the truck are greeted by Tim and his wife, Antoinette, who have dinner and a bed waiting. The house was built in the late 1920s or early '30s. It served as home for Greg as

At our Loup City, Nebraska farm, Antoinette photographs Tim as he tends to a cow that is more than happy to receive a treat.

he raised cattle there for a few years. In was recently refurbished by Tim and Antoinette, after being trashed by a renter. In the farm yard, is a high wind break of various species of trees providing shelter for cattle while the cows are at "winter camp." The trees also provide a home for a variety of song birds during the spring and summer months.

For those individuals who continually say "there is nothing but flat land in Kansas and Nebraska and absolutely nothing to see," I want them to know how wrong they are. When I first met Art, I told him "The only way to see Nebraska was at night with your eyes closed." I certainly have had to "eat my words" as making the trip from the ranch to the farm has proved me WRONG! There is so much to see and the sights change as do the seasons. The farm has the highest point in Sherman County and was a terrific place to observe the eclipse of the sun a few years ago.

Trucking Experiences

"Do you think you can drive a truck with stick shift and how about one pulling a loaded cattle trailer?" This was one of the first questions both Art and Greg asked me. My answer was, "Why not!" I must admit, I really did not realize what the future would be but I quickly found out.

Gopher/Go For

This is a word or words when said fast means two entirely different things, but in both cases, a person needs to react. When the word "gopher" is said, it usually means a 13 striped ground squirrel is at hand. When the phrase "Go for" is yelled out, it means the farmer/rancher needs the wife to drop whatever she is doing, get into the nearest road worthy vehicle and make a trip to the closest town to get whatever item is needed at the time. Of course, this all depends on the time of the year and the projects currently being undertaken. I always thought I should have a license plate with "Go 4" on it but soon realized other farm/ranch wives had already laid claim to this.

For me the "Go for" began the first day on the ranch when we were commuting from Denver and were quite unprepared for anything and everything. Fortunately, there was a Mini-Mart a mile and a half away where I could and would go for sandwiches and cold drinks. When the fence building began, it meant I must drive fifteen miles to the hardware store for more string, a yardstick to measure the depth of the post hole, gloves, spray paint, and, oh yes, on the way back, pick up some sandwiches and more cold drinks.

As time went on and the ranch became home to cows and calves, the "Go for" meant longer trips such as driving 45 miles to Colorado Springs for ear tags to use to identify the cows and calves, or for more rubber gloves, or vaccines from the animal supply outlet. Of course, it always meant a stop someplace to pick up lunch. As the herd grew in number, so did the demand for buckets, tubs, paddles used when separating the animals, gloves, warm clothes, tablets for cleaning the water tanks, lag bolts, tools, stock salt, mineral supplement and of course, lunch.

There were also short trips of seven and one-half miles to the veterinarian clinic for health papers required when the cows were being transported to Nebraska for "winter camp" or when a special medicine was needed to treat a cow or calf.

On one "Go for" occasion, I had to drive to Grand Island, Nebraska, a 465-mile trip to pick up a semen tank. This trip would take two days so I had my friend, Nancy, ride along. The trip was done by car which had G.P.S. so there was no danger of getting lost. The funny part though was when the driver (me) and the G.P.S. disagreed on which exit to use. Since I had been a Geography major in college, I knew how to read a map and exactly how to reach the final destination. After passing three exits suggested by the G.P.S., the system was cancelled and the two of us went happily on our way. When we turned off the Interstate, it was late in the afternoon and way past time for lunch so what was needed now was a motel and dinner. These were both found quickly and we were also close to a nice shopping mall. Who's to say, "women would turn down a shopping chance?" The next morning, with written directions in hand, we proceeded to the desired location, picked up the semen tank, full of frozen embryos, and began the trek back to Colorado. I thought I should have a sign on the top of the car, not "wide load" but one stating "Future Babies On Board." This "Go for" trip was a fun one, not only did we have lunch together, but breakfast, lunch and dinner.

No matter the situation, the wife is always the "Go for" but for her, it is always beneficial. I got to meet new people, see new sights along the roadside, and did not have to cook. Of course, there were times when my cooking was stopped midstream thus having to be restarted or reheated. Life on the farm/ranch makes everyday a new experience.

Trip to the Feed Mill

"We need feed today and I am busy, so could you go and get it?" These words were said quite early in the ranching days by Art to me. Art was busy putting a water tank in position on a poured cement base in what would be the northeast pasture. He was being helped by a neighbor who had a full-time construction job elsewhere but was willing to help this poor struggling rancher. The "Why not" was quickly replaced with "I guess so," was my response. I was still learning how to drive the truck without having a nervous breakdown. So here again the red pickup with the "stick" gear shift was put to use. Now, the feed mill was about two and a half hours away from the ranch but the animals were being given special feed and this was the only place around that would mix it for us. I started out early in the morning with what I thought was plenty of time. Going to the mill meant going through Denver on the Interstate but traveling in the morning, the journey went well. I got to the mill and was getting loaded, but this is where things got interesting. The bed of the truck was quickly filled with feed bags but there were still more to go. "Where to put them?" In the cab was the logical answer so the cab was completely filled. It was hard- but not impossible-just hard to get to the stick shift so as to be in the correct gear. Everything went well except I had to drive back through Denver and by now time was against me. The traffic was getting heavy and slowing down meant having to shift gears. This meant working around the 50-pound bags of feed. To those of you who have had this challenge, you know with what I was dealing. The experience ended well, actually better than I expected. I got home with the truck before dark and fortunately without any flat tires or storms. When I got out of the truck, I found it was hard to open my fingers as I had held such a tight grip on the steering wheel. My knees were also a bit wobbly from having to use the clutch and brake so often but I was gaining experience. It was after this episode that a better plan of attack was garnered. Back roads to the feed mill were found with very little traffic and absolutely no driving on the Interstate. This new route is much less strenuous and the scenery more beautiful and interesting. The feed is now loaded into a cattle trailer which definitely holds more than the "old red pickup" so fewer trips are required.

Bringing Hay from Nebraska

Another truck driving tale was when hay from our farm in Nebraska was needed in Colorado. The farm in Loup City was purchased many years earlier by Art and his brother. Rob. It was used primarily for growing corn, beans and hay. After we moved to Colorado, Greg began living there raising cattle of his own as well as growing alfalfa hay. This time the "red pickup" was pulling a 20-foot cattle trailer. This trip was to take about six and a half hours depending on how comfortable the unseasoned driver would be. It was at the time when car phones were a relatively new object and the "red pickup" was equipped with such an object. It was not a flip one but, back in the dark ages, it was known as a "bag phone," certainly not as easy to operate as the newer models. I started out with everything going well, the truck was driving well and the trailer was pulling easily. As I was about to get on a different road, the phone rang. At the other end was Art. "How are you doing?" My answer was "I was doing fine until the phone rang." Fortunately, I had pulled off the main road into a parking spot so was able to answer all the questions and assure the concerned husband that everything was OK. I made the turn, got on the Interstate, crossed the state line from Colorado into Nebraska and after many miles made the turn to another two-way road leading to North Platte. Once again, the phone rang just as I was driving through a town that did not have straight streets. This time it was Greg asking, "Where are you and how long before you get here?" Once again, my answer was same, "I was doing fine until the phone rang." The answer was short and I made it through the town and went on my way for the next two hours after which I arrived at the farm. The next day the trailer was loaded with hay and I was on my way back to Colorado. One slight problem. I needed fuel so since I really didn't know how to back up the truck with the attached trailer, I had to carefully pull into the filling station and drive correctly to the gas pump so as to guarantee a forward departure. Just another lesson to be learned!

Transporting a New Bull

Time went on and I became more proficient in driving the truck. The "Why not" and the "I guess so" now became "I KNOW I CAN!" The red pickup was now being used primarily as a snow plow and had been replaced with a larger new 2005 Ford 350 flatbed truck stick shift model. It was in this truck that the next trucking event took place. A bull had been purchased in Nebraska and I was elected to take him to our farm in Loup City. So off I went on this mission driving on unknown route. Everything went well until I drove past the driveway where the bull was being kept. I still did not know how to back up while pulling the trailer so help was needed. I called the office where the bull was and asked if someone could come and help me. They sent another female who really didn't know how to back up either but she did say "There is a circular drive down the road just a way, drive there and you can easily make the turnaround." I did just that and while waiting for the bull to be loaded into the trailer, I found out that none of the women employed there knew how to successfully back up a truck and trailer either. All had a good laugh not at me but with me. The bull was loaded so driver, truck and trailer continued on our way, up and down hills, shifting and down shifting smoothly, not to upset the bull. End of story, the bull was in fine shape, eager to get out and to find feed and water. The truck and trailer made it back to Colorado successfully and this time, I was much calmer at the end of my escapade.

Foggy Day Driving

Another experience happened when returning cows from Nebraska (winter camp). The cows are taken to the family farm in Nebraska where there are corn fields on the property. Here corn is found on the ground that has not been totally gleaned when harvested. In addition, the leaves on the corn stalks provide additional food for the cows. This provides adequate nutrition for the pregnant cows during the winter months. However, if there is snow covering the ground, hay will be provided for the cows. On this particular trip, I was in the smaller truck pulling a trailer which would hold nine cows and Art was in the larger Ford 550 pulling a much larger trailer holding twelve cows. Both trailers were filled with pregnant cows. It was an extremely foggy day so driving conditions were not the best. We were in Kansas on a two-lane road which was heavily traveled by huge cattle trucks taking cattle to nearby feedlots and they were driving like they had a mission-which of course, they did. Art was the front truck and was driving away from me. All at once, he could not see me in his rear view mirror. So he, of course, was worried and got on the dreaded phone. "Where are you? I can't see you." The answer was, "I am fine. I can see you and I am driving the conditions." The phone went dead and the trip was continued in silence.

The Most Disastrous Trip

This trip was on the same two-lane road in Kansas with the same two trucks and trailers. This time I was in the lead truck when all of a sudden Art drove around me, pulled to the side of the road and stopped. Immediately I knew something must be wrong. When driving a truck pulling a trailer a quick stop is definitely not in order so I slowly pulled in behind him. He came back to the truck and said "You are going to have to stay close behind me because my running lights are not working." "Oh, my gosh" was the reply as once again there were cattle trucks using the road and going very fast. So, being a careful woman driver, I used the emergency flasher lights on my truck and trailer, hoping to warn the big haulers that the two small trucks with trailers were in distress. This trip was to be remembered as "the trip from hell!" I was low on fuel and hoping I could make it to the next town? I tried to call Art but we were in a dead zone so no communication. I tried getting his attention by flashing my lights but to no avail. I continued driving on, always getting closer to the town and gas pumps all the time thinking "if I can make it to the main road, it will be closer to town and there is a place there to pull off in case I have to wait for help." It was starting to get dark but so far so good. I got on U.S. 36, and Norton was in sight, the fuel tank was not completely empty, so all was well. I pulled into the filling station, got out the truck and gave a big sigh of relief. I had pulled correctly to the pump so no backing up was required- Smile! I knew how to fill my own fuel tank so no help needed there. The tank was

The two trucks with their trailers involved in the most disastrous trip.

Ruth had to follow Art when his running lights failed to work.

full, so that mission accomplished. I got back into the truck and drove across the street where Art was waiting, also refueling at another station. Here is the second problem. As Art pulled away from the pump, he hit the post guarding the pump. This damaged the rim and tore up the tire. OK. We have a spare rim and tire along with the equipment to fix the problem. By that time, it was completely dark, raining and getting cold. With the possibility of failing lights, it definitely was not advisable to drive on. As a result, we spent night in a local motel.

Next morning the caravan started out, driving to Art's home town of Minden, Nebraska, where the light problem could be and was supposedly solved. After a couple of hours, the trip continued north to the farm where the pregnant cows were waiting. Our son, Tim, who lived in Indiana at that time, was waiting to help drive the smaller truck and trailer filled with the pregnant cows back to Colorado. It was in the middle of February, a beautiful sunny day, the cows were loaded and all was well. I was riding with Tim and all of a sudden there was a screeching sound and a light came on indicating a problem with the trailer. A stop was made in Kearney at a trailer repair shop where they thought they had solved the problem, but not so. A few miles down the highway, that horrible noise sounded again. Once again, the caravan drove back to Minden, back to the Ford dealer where it was decided the only way to eliminate the noise was to disconnect the trailer brakes. This done, once again, we were on our way. By now it was afternoon and we still had a six-hour drive ahead of us. With both trailers loaded with cattle, there was no option but to drive on. This went well until once again, Art called saying, "My lights are gone again." Everybody stopped, Art got new fuses with extra spares, just in case, and on we went. It was getting later and darker but the home driveway was in sight. Both trucks and trailers made it up the driveway and down to the barn. When we pulled up to the gate where we emptied our cargo, the cows got out immediately knowing they were home and went non stop for water and the feed bunks. The six-hour drive had turned into a ten hour one because of all the stops but all ended well and this adventure makes for another good story.

The Importance of Cell Phones

Not all trucking experiences directly involve me. There was one time when three trucks pulling trailers, of various sizes, were taking steers to a feedlot in northeastern Colorado. This was shortly after cell phones came on the market and while just about everyone had one, the range was somewhat limited. Art told me that I also needed a cell phone to which I replied "Why?" "So, I can call you in case of an emergency" was the reply. The conversation was concluded when I replied "When you are trucking, I am at home always in reach of the land line."

This was proven when the three trucks were well on the road and Art called home saying "We've had a tire go bad. Can you find the closest tire dealer?" No sooner had I hung up the phone than Greg called, "I can't reach Dad and I don't know where I am supposed to take the steers." Using my ever-faithful land line, I made some calls, first to friends who knew the owners of the feedlot as well as their address, so that problem was solved. By the time I got back to Greg, he had already asked someone in a service station for directions and was well on his way to make the delivery. The tire problem meant looking at a map to locate the nearest town and then calling a tire distributor to see if tires were even available. Success! The stay-at-home telephone operator took care of the problem-tires were purchased, steers were delivered and all three trucks returned home safely.

Help!

Another one of the stay-at-home trips for me found me answering the ever-faithful land-line phone. "We've gone through two tires" said the desperate voice on the other end. "Call ahead to Flagler and find tires." Once again, the land line was put to use and the problem was solved. On that trip four trailer tires were changed before returning to the home driveway. After watching tires being changed on NASCAR racers, I decided a twenty-eight Volt impact wrench would make a terrific Christmas present for Art. I even made a canvas bag to put it in. It's place of importance is right behind the driver's seat. It makes changing the tire much quicker and easier, especially when the trailer is loaded with cattle.

Cow Fall Trip to Nebraska

When trucking cattle to Nebraska in the fall, the scenario was Art and possibly a friend would take the first load of cows, leaving me home to feed the ones left behind. The reverse would be in the spring when I would ride along for the first load and then stay at home to feed and watch the maternity ward. The trips would start out early in the morning, usually before breakfast, so a tradition of "breakfast sandwiches" was begun. This was long before Jimmy Dean micro-wave sandwiches were on the market. The hot egg McMuffins were put in a thermal bag along with a pint jar filled with very hot water. When the truck got on the interstate and all the necessary shifting was completed, the sandwiches along with cartons of orange juice were made available. When loaded with cattle, the trucks only stop for fuel and this does not mean fuel for the drivers. I claim my back side sees more of the road than my front as I serve the food which always needs to be recovered from the back seat. Get the picture? Art claims our homemade breakfast sandwiches are far better than any on those bought while in route. Cheaper too!

Outside Help is Appreciated

"We'll be right there" was the response given to our plea for assistance. This experience exemplifies how great mid-western ranchers are and how they are always willing to help others.

We had just purchased 20 heifers at the sale barn in Ogallala, Nebraska, and the heifers were to be taken 75 miles away to a veterinarian in Bridgeport, Nebraska. The heifers would spend the winter there and be artificially inseminated in the spring. The trailer was loaded at the sale barn and we started on our way. We had one truck and trailer but all of a sudden, the truck stopped, "deader than a doornail." What to do? Fortunately, we were only about a half mile out of the town where there happened to be a Ford dealer. The dealer was called but said the tow truck was out of town. They would not be able to tow both the truck and loaded trailer back because of the heavy load. What were the other options? Art got out of the truck and started walking back to the sale barn when a driver stopped to give him a ride. In the meantime, Olsons, the people who had originally owned the heifers were called. They lived about 28 miles up the road and if needed would be glad to come and get the animals. When Art got to the sale barn, there was a young man who had a flatbed truck and was willing and able to come to the rescue. The first thing to be done was to pull the truck away from the trailer so the rescue truck could back in and get connected to the trailer. Mission accomplished. Now the Ford dealer could easily tow the truck to the garage. The rescue truck with the heifers in the trailer were returned to the sale barn and put back in the pen they had just relinquished. They were given hay, water, and bedded down for however long it might take.

When the truck got to the garage, the mechanic immediately started his investigation only to find that a part was needed which would have to come from Denver. This was on a Friday. It meant we would spend the weekend in a motel. Not to worry, the Ford dealer would give us a truck to use in the meantime. Back to the original motel where a room was available. Not only was it Friday but it was also Valentine's Day. Art had a fraternity brother living in Gothenburg, a town not too far away, so a call was made setting up a dinner date. This was great except that Jan and Jerry lived in the Central Time Zone and we were in the Mountain Time Zone. The restaurant did not kick out the first arrivals for the five o'clock dinner as they patiently waited an hour for us to arrive at what was five o'clock mountain time. What a laugh everyone had as well as having great conversations and dinner. Saturday morning arrived and with it was a telephone call from the Ford dealer. "Your truck is ready!" How about that for customer service for people who had never been there before? Back to the sale barn where the heifers were waiting. They were loaded into the trailer and when we offered to pay, the answer was "There is no charge." It is circumstances like these that make us say we are proud to be ranchers. The heifers were delivered, spent the winter in Bridgeport and came home to Colorado in the spring where they delivered their baby calves. Once again, all is well that ends well!

Superman of the Highway

Another example of kindness was after we had driven a new Ford F450 truck to Lincoln, Nebraska for a funeral. On the way back, we picked up a twenty-four-foot trailer loaded with square bales of hay weighing 20,000 pounds. All was going well until we stopped to make a right turn onto a highway in Kansas. The truck stopped-never to go again-at least at that point. The Ford company, who supposedly provided road-side service, was called and they said someone would be there shortly. WRONG! We sat in the truck for over an hour, all the time trying to get help but to no avail. All of a sudden, here was a Kansas State Patrol car pulling up in the front of the truck. After asking what the problem was, he said "I think I can help you." Out came a short rope which he attached to the truck and the patrol car. He then said, "Since you are ranchers, I'm sure you've had experience being towed. I will lead and you control the brakes from your end." The patrol car was a Ford Crown Victoria. After some spinning of his wheels, the patrolman, truck and trailer were on our way. All of a sudden, a car, going quite fast, passed the slow-moving vehicles. When the driver realized she had just passed a Patrol Car, her speed immediately became much slower. What a laugh we had. When the trip of six miles was over and the truck/trailer had been deposited in a large truck parking facility, we were told that the patrolman had called ahead and obtained motel reservations for us. We never knew the name of the patrolman but to us he is known as "Superman of the Highway." The woman who had been driving the fast-going car was also at the motel and said she had been stopped for speeding at the previous town and had been given a warning. The next morning, we were rescued by a tow truck and putting the ailing truck on the flatbed, leaving the trailer filled with hay in the parking lot, we were off to the nearest Ford dealer in McCook, Nebraska. Funny part of the story is that the truck driver knew he was overweight with the Ford F450 as his load, so he just waved as he went past the weigh station on the side of the road. We had to leave the truck as it was a Friday and the needed parts would not be available until Monday. We were finally given a "loaner" so we could get home which was most important as we were hosting a Christmas party for twenty-four friends the next day. This episode ends with the car being returned to the dealer, the needed repairs being accomplished, and the truck was returned home. The hay was rescued the following week.

Weather Makes Trucking Interesting

One of the first cattle hauling adventures involved the "red pickup" and the red twenty-foot trailer loaded with nine cows going to family land south of Minden, Nebraska. We were well along in the journey when Greg called saying we were running into ice. The problem was that we were already more than half way along and so far, the weather was good. So, on we went. With good luck, we made the dropping off area, unloaded the pregnant cows and started back to Colorado. Not So Good! Five miles on a gravel road and then a turn onto the main highway where we were greeted with a layer of "Black Ice." Question, "What do we do now?" My response was quite simple. "Call your mother and see if she would like company for at least tonight." The call was made, the trailer turned around and instead of going south, we were now heading north for twelve miles to spend the night in the nice warm home of Art's mother. The trip was continued the next day but only after the ice was melted and the highway safe for a truck pulling a trailer. The saying in Colorado is "If you don't like the weather, wait five minutes."

This does not always prove to be true; we were returning from a cattle sale in Ogallala, Nebraska where we were in one truck and Greg was in the second. We suddenly ran into dense fog and the closer we got to home, the worse the weather got. When pulling into our driveway, we were met with ice. We were in the Ford 550 pulling the thirty-foot aluminum trailer and all of a sudden, the trailer started sliding backwards, pulling the truck with it. The trailer was at right angles to the driveway and the truck was off to the side in the ditch. Greg was in the F350 pulling the twenty-foot trailer. He said "I am going to drive through the pasture and get to the barn. I can bring the Excursion back and we'll unload the bags then." Only problem, I had the car keys in my purse and only remembered that after Greg had already driven away. Fortunately, Tom and Melody McCreight had gone to the sale with us, leaving their new F150 four-wheel drive truck at the barn. Greg and Tom rescued our stranded bodies and everyone was saved! Dinner, although sparse, was served at the house with Tom and Melody spending the night because of the horrible road conditions. We all enjoyed playing a table game so a bad situation turned into a great evening with fun for all.

One observation made by both of us is that on all the trucking trips, the cows remain quiet in the trailers. Upon reaching their destination and the tailgate is lowered into a corn field in Nebraska, the cow front legs come to the ground first, the head follows, all the time looking down for corn, even before getting completely out of the trailer. After jumping out of the trailer, it seems to me they instinctively know where to find water and immediately head in that direction.

My other observation is when the cows return from Nebraska in the spring and the trailer stops at the unloading gate, the cows moo as if they know they are home and fresh green grass is waiting for them. These animals seem to have a terrific memory but who am I to say?

Feed Trip

This story includes all aspects of ranching, feed, weather, Bungee cords, Ratchet straps, tarps, Duct tape, and days of togetherness. We were driving the Ford 550 to Nebraska to pick up feed. Our cows are so special, they are fed only the best rations which are obtained from a feed mill in Art's home town of Minden. The day was a beautiful sun shiny day in late January. The roads were good and timing was such that we could stop and have lunch with fraternity brother, Ray Kelly and his wife, Viola. By the time we reached our designated lodging I was not feeling well but I thought I would be fine by morning when we would load up and head back home. This was not to be the case so Art went to Minden, loaded up the feed and returned to the motel. Here is where things got interesting. There was weather coming in.

The feed was in bags on the back of the truck and would be exposed to the weather. Tarps were needed to protect the cargo. A trip was made to the local lumber/hardware/equipment store (Menards). Tarps were purchased as were more Bungee cords and Ratchet straps, (another new term) and of course, lots of Duct tape. Bungee cord, was not a new term at this time as I had learned about this quite early in my ranching days. I had been sent to a ranch equipment store to purchase this item. When asked, by the clerk, what size I needed, I had to confess I really wasn't sure what I was looking for, let alone needing to know a size. I found out quickly that a Bungee cord is an elastic cord, composed of one or more elastic strands, then covered with a woven cotton. This cord of various lengths, has hooks on both ends and the stretching of the elastic depends on the size of the project. In the case of securing the feed which had already been covered by tarps, the Bungee cords would be used to tie the tarps down to the side of the panels on the truck. This task was accomplished but when the weather report included high wind and snow, it was decided Rachet straps were needed. Just another learning lesson for me.

Ratchet straps have many different names, such as, "Cargo tie-downs," "Wrench strap," or just a "tie down strap." These heavy-duty straps are seen quite often on semi-trucks with high, extremely heavy loads. They are connected to the sides of the trucks, in a roll when not in use. For ranchers, these heavy-duty straps are used when delivering the large round hay bales. There may be as many as 10 straps going from side to side of the truck bed over the bales and two or more from the front of the flatbed trailer to the rear, guaranteeing that the bales will not be sliding around. In this case, our load was not high nor that heavy but security was important. To accomplish this task, I would stand on one side of the truck making sure the 2 ½ to 3-inch steel hook would be correctly and securely placed under the side rail of the flatbed. The strap would be thrown over the covered feed so Art could secure the hook on the other side. When both hooks are in place, the rachet mechanism is used to tighten the strap. Prior to this adventure, my job was usually to rewind

Only the driver knows for sure what is on this truck.

the strap and secure it in place with a Bungee cord, and put it back in the cab of the truck ready for future emergencies. As we were hurriedly completing this project, the wind became a problem. So now to completely safeguard our cargo, it was decided to use Duct tape on any and all loose ends. We certainly did not want any tarp flying off as we were driving down the Interstate.

Three days later, this truck with its cargo, completely covered with tarps, taped together, tied down with Rachet straps and Bungee cords with not a clue as what might be under all that covering was heading west, homeward bound. It was fun watching the faces of the passengers in cars as they passed the truck. They were probably wondering what in the world was so valuable that it had to be so severely covered. We will never tell but the feed definitely stayed dry and was truly appreciated by the hungry cows.

An Unusual Trucking Experience

How many women have ever gone to a bridal shower in a truck pulling a cattle trailer? This tale began as a normal bridal shower experience but things quickly changed. First, when Art realized I would be going to his hometown of Minden, where I would be using his sister, Joan's, home to host the shower for the wife to be of his grandnephew, Chris, he said, "Well, as long as you are already there, you can take the truck and trailer and bring the bull back from Loup City." Second, although the date for the shower had been agreed upon and the invitation mailed, the bride-to-be could not be in attendance. This changed everything and it became an "Absentee Shower" with the honoree attending via Skype. The invitees were asked to bring their gifts unwrapped so all could see what the guest of honor would be receiving. This proved to be quite interesting as most of the guests had been married for at least twenty-five years or more. There were comments, such as, "I could certainly use that," or "What is that and what is it used for?" Wrapping supplies were provided by the hostess and instead of games, prizes were awarded for the most beautifully wrapped gift or the most original one. It truly was a once in a lifetime experience but the day was enjoyed by all present.

One of the invited guests happened to be my dear, close friend, named Nancy, who agreed to ride "shot gun" in the truck. Nancy was also a city girl, from New Jersey and seeing the landscapes across Kansas and Nebraska was a new adventure. I had driven this route many times, so was able to identify different crops in the roadside fields. To those who say there is nothing to see but flat land, grass and cattle, they must not be really interested as there are fields of corn, soybeans, milo, and forage sorghum which is harvested as roughage for cattle.

Nancy was also an important part of the trip. The cake being served at the party had been baked and decorated by a longtime friend of the groom in Bertrand, Nebraska. We stopped in Bertrand, picked up the cake and Nancy very carefully held it for the last forty-five miles of the trip to Minden.

The day after the shower, all the beautifully wrapped gifts were put in the "nose" of the cattle trailer so they could be opened by the bride and groom at a later date in Colorado. The bull was loaded in the trailer, but quite a way from the gifts. Everyone and everything made it back to Colorado in fine condition. It would be interesting to know how many other women have had to drive a truck pulling a cattle trailer to a bridal shower. There does not seem to be any dull moments in my life.

Ruth and best friend Nancy, preparing to leave on a bridal-shower trip.

WHEN THE SPERM AND EGG MEET

Not only did I have a lot to learn about ranching but after our first church school picnic, we realized from the questions asked, that others were truly interested about all facets of ranching. One question frequently asked was, "What is the life span of a cow and how many calves will one produce?" That was a simple question to answer. "We'll keep her as long as she has teeth so she can eat and produce milk for her calf." Another question was, "How and where do you get replacements for the cows?" Here again, it was a rather simple answer. "The calves produced the first year of calving were all black Angus so all the heifers were kept to add to the herd. The following year, the cows mated with a Hereford bull which produced the F1 cross breed heifers which were sold to other people for replacements in their herds. For us to get the black Angus replacements, we needed to either buy an Angus bull or do artificial insemination or what is commonly called "AIing."

To answer all the questions from the previous year, Greg gave a short seminar to a room full of people consisting of doctors, nurses, and scientists from various fields. The audience had grown so the barn became a laboratory as Greg showed them all the equipment he uses for the AI procedure. This included the semen tank holding the semen straws kept in liquid nitrogen. He also explained how he injects the straws into the cow. In short, he gave a full course on artificial insemination in a few minutes. Maybe it was more than what they really wanted to know but they were the ones who had asked the questions and Greg was certainly the one to give them the answers. For those of you without knowledge of artificial insemination, it is a very interesting subject and I hope your curiosity is so aroused that you will continue reading. Every time I heard Greg tell about it, I learned even more and we are never too old to learn.

At this time with political correctness, AI means "Artificial Intelligence" but to a person dealing with livestock, AI means "Artificial Insemination." The purpose of artificial insemination is twofold. Most importantly, it allows the ranchers to genetically pick from a long list of bulls the one who best fits into a particular program. On Eagles Nest Ranch, the cows are moderate framed black Angus so the bulls chosen have a certain criteria based on size, predicted calving weight and body structure. By being able to breed most of the cows on day one it allows for the breeding and calving to be completed within a sixty-day period. Of course, there

Cow in the head gate ready for artificial insemination.

are exceptions but for the most part, this program works quite well.

For it to be successful, it starts with the synchronization of the cows. They will be brought into chute in the barn three days before the start of breeding. After a cow has had a calf, it will take her six weeks to come into estrus meaning she will be ovulating and will be ready for breeding. At Eagles Nest Ranch, this means by the 25th of June, 85 - 95% will be cycling—of course, not all cows will fit into this schedule as a few have calved later. The cows will all be given a shot of Lutalyse, a drug which causes the corpus luteum (CL) to regress. The corpus luteum produces hormones that help maintain pregnancy provided the cow conceives. When the CL is destroyed, the cow's system knows she is not pregnant. She will then come into

Greg doing the insemination.

heat three days later and will be ready to be bred. This synchronization only works in cows that are cycling. At any given time, about half the cows have a functional corpus luteum so the expectation is that half of the cycling cows will be ready for breeding.

At the time of injection, a very visible mark in put on the cow's tail head with a yellow paint stick. When a cow comes into heat, she will be mounted by other cows removing the mark. The cows are continuously watched during the day and when the mark is gone, it is a sign she has been in heat. When the egg pushes out of the ovary, it is painful and the cow will stand still, thus allowing the bull to service her. It takes approximately twelve hours for the semen from the bull and the egg from the cow to meet. When using AI, the semen is deposited past the cervix, thereby meeting the egg at a much shorter time period. So generally, a cow is inseminated by AI 12 hours after she comes into estrus. When the egg is fertilized, it embeds itself in the uterine horn and when settled, the embryo will start to form. AI or natural service does not always insure pregnancy but it usually successful 65% of the time.

Insemination Procedure

Once the technician knows the cow/heifer is in heat, she is brought into the barn, and put in the head gate. A straw of semen, the size of a swizzle stick is put in a 98-degree water bath for a minute to thaw and activate the sperm. While this is happening, the technician is putting on a plastic arm glove. A French straw gun is put inside his shirt so it will be the same temperature as the semen. The semen straw is retrieved from the water bath, put into the end of the gun, the end of the straw is clipped off and a disposable plastic sheath is placed over the gun, thereby holding everything in place. The gun is put back in the technician shirt to maintain the temperature. OB lube or detergent is in the palm of the gloved hand and the technician goes to the waiting cow. The tail of the cow is lifted, the lubricated gloved hand is rubbed over the cows rectum, thereby lubricating the technicians arm for easy insertion into the rectum. The straw gun is then put in the reproductive track, and when it gets to the opening of the cervix, the gloved hand manipulates the gun through the cervix which has folds pointing back. After passing the gun through the folds, the technician will feel the tip of the gun passing the inside of the cervix and the semen is ejected from the gun into the uterus. The technician pulls out his arm, removes the glove and the procedure begins all over in the next waiting animal. Hopefully in 283 days, there will be a black female calf on the ground. Of course, it is not always a female. Generally, the number of males and females are quite even.

On a much lighter side, Greg was AIing cows and it was beginning to get dark outside. Even though the procedure was being done in the barn, without thinking I asked him if he needed the lights turned on. His answer was "Mom, I don't need the lights as I sure can't see inside the cow. My work is done only by feel." Oh well, just another lesson to be learned by the city girl.

Although the AI procedure is time consuming for the technician, it does make the calving period tighter. More cows will be giving birth within the first three weeks. If a bull is involved, he can only service five cows in one day, where the technician will do as many as his arm can withstand.

Purebred breeders will do artificial insemination to utilize high reputation bulls where large commercial breeders have the option depending on their desired results.

Semen

There are many companies providing semen, however, for Eagles Nest Ranch, the semen is usually purchased from ABS (American Breeding Service) out of Wisconsin. Every year they publish a catalog listing available semen from about 100 different Angus bulls as well as from other breeds. This catalog contains extensive genetic information on each bull. The bull whose semen the breeder desires is selected based on his physical characteristics, blood line (ancestry) and genetic information. The breeder is very careful to select bulls not related to the cow so as to prevent any inbreeding.

The semen from reputation bulls is sold by the straw, costing $10 to $40 each. This is shipped to the ranch in a tank cooled with liquid nitrogen and when it arrives, it is transferred into the ranch "semen tank" which will hold 240 straws. This tank is refilled with liquid nitrogen three times a year or every fourth month.

The synchronized cows, not bred with Angus semen, will be inseminated with semen collected from the owners black Hereford bulls. To collect semen, the bulls are taken to a sire service, Rocky Mountain Sire Service, close to Denver where they will stay for two to three days, The semen will be collected, diluted with an egg wash (the same mixture as used for French Toast), and then put in the straws. Each straw contains approximately two drops of diluted semen. Generally, one collection will produce 150 straws.

To protect the privacy of all bovine, there will be no further discussion on how the semen is collected. Of course, one can always Goggle it!

Pregnancy Check

This procedure is similar to insemination, although here the object is to feel the fetus in the reproductive tract through the intestine wall. If a fetus is felt and is the size of a mouse, the cow will be classified as one month pregnant. If it is the size of a small dog, it will be four months.

Dr. Clint Kinsell was doing the pregnancy check for Eagles Nest Ranch and he kept saying "four months" which left the ranchers thinking they would not be leaving the ranch anytime five months later but, calves like humans, come when they are ready. The funny part of this tale is when Art and Greg had taken the bull to the vet clinic for a fertility check and when Clint was conducting the rectal exam, he called out "four months!" Oh well, everyone has to have a faux pas at one time or another.

Answers to Questions

Some of you might be wondering how Greg was qualified to be a technician for the artificial insemination. He attended Purdue University in Indiana where he had a Physiology and Reproductive of Livestock class which covered all aspects of the

AI techniques. When he began doing the work for the ranch, he attended a week-long refresher course at Graham School, Inc. in Kansas. This Herdsman's school covered not only reproduction but also nutrition concerns to better prepare the cow for insemination.

As far as what part we play in the operation, it is quite simple. Art brings the cows into the barn from the corral and pushes the next in line into the head gate. Greg takes over from there. When the procedure is finished, Art makes sure the cow goes back to the corral. For me, my secretarial training is put to use by recording which semen was injected into which cow. This is important as semen from six different bulls, depending on the genetic background, will be used eliminating all possibility of inbreeding.

Cross Breeding

The goal of Eagles Nest Ranch was to raise "first cross heifers" which would be sold to other farmers/ranchers as replacement females for their herds. To achieve this, the bull must be from another breed. After a great deal of research, it was decided Polled Hereford bulls would be the best pick to breed our Angus cows.

The Hereford breed originated in Herefordshire, England and has a reputation for gaining weight by eating grass alone, which was a perfect choice for the Colorado pastures. Early records show a Hereford bull winning the Grand Champion at the first Royal Show in England in 1839. Statesman, Henry Clay, imported the first two heifers and one bull to Kentucky in 1817. In 1825, a bull and heifer were presented to the Massachusetts Society for the Promotion of Agriculture by an Admiral of the Royal Navy. In 1839-40, more Herefords were imported and in 1898, the breeding program to produce Polled (hornless) Herefords began in Des Moines, Iowa.

The Herefords originally had a red coat with various colors of red, with characteristic white faces, white bellies and some white on the legs. They are known to be docile and continue the reputation of being able to gain weight on grassland.

We began the cross-breeding by using the black Angus heifer calves from their original thirty-seven cows and mating them with a Polled Hereford bull. This resulted in the production of black white-faced animals, commonly called "Black Baldys." Animals produced from this cross have "hybrid vigor" which means they possess the best qualities of both breeds. When the female offspring are sold to other ranchers/farmers, they will be bred to a third breed and all offspring will be sold as "terminal crosses."

For the most part, over the years, we had good crops of "black baldys" but every once in a while, a red calf would appear. This happens because some Angus cows have recessive red genes instead of two dominate black genes so when mated with a Hereford bull who has two red genes, half the time, the calf will be red. It does not mean this heifer calf is any different structurally or genetically different but for a buyer who wants continuity in his black Angus herd, a red one will not fit the bill. Both red and black Herefords are selected for the amount of pigment around their eyes which helps in preventing "pink eye," an infection of the cornea.

This problem has been solved because over the past ten years, a black Polled Hereford breed has been developed. With the genetic research conducted by Greg, the ranch now produces only AngusXBlackHereford F1 calves.

Embryo Transfer (ET)

Here again I had to learn new terms, such as "donor, recipient, flushing, and loading. In doing research on the subject of embryo transfer I found it involves moving a live embryo from one animal to another (ET). This procedure was first performed and recorded by Walter Heape in 1890 as he was experimenting with Belgium Angora rabbits. In the 1930s, ET was begun using sheep and goats but it was not really successful until the 1950s when non-surgical success by Jim Davison was reported from Cambridge, England. In the United States, the first commercial transfers were done surgically in the early 1970'a but non-surgical methods were developed in the late 1970s. After this, the practice using non-surgical methods grew in popularity.

The first step in the ET procedure and probably the most important is the selection of a genetically outstanding donor cow. She should be reproductive sound and have an appropriate body condition at the time of ET. There is quite an established criteria to be followed to have a successful operation.

Second is a time-consuming process which involves "superovulation" of the donor cow. It involves a process where hormones are injected twice daily for four days at the middle or near end of the donor cows' normal estrous cycle. Cows/heifers can release as many as ten or more viable eggs at one time.

Third is insemination when the superovulated cow comes into heat (standing estrus), a specialized technician will inject one straw of high-quality semen into the body of the uterus just in front of the cervix (the same procedure as in artificial insemination). Six hours later, two straws will be injected and six hours later, one more straw be injected.

Fourth involves "flushing." Seven days later the technician will use a saline solution to fill the cows' reproductive tract allowing the solution to come back out with the eggs to be collected. The technician, using an established standard criteria, will microscopically examine and sort the fertilized eggs. The embryos will be classified according to their quality, from the top being excellent/good, through fair and poor to the lowest category being dead or degenerating. Once again, following a set criteria, the embryos are evaluated according to developmental stages. If they are of a high quality and have at least four cells or more, they may be frozen. If not, they may be utilized by immediately injecting it into a recipient cow who has been synchronized with the donor cow. This is important because the donor and recipient must be at the same stage of the estrus cycle period due to the timing of the development of the corpus luteum (CL) which happens seven days later when the embryo is implanted.

The transfer involves loading the embryo into an insemination straw which is done under a microscope with a syringe. The technician must be blessed with dexterity, patience and hopefully, a lot of previous experience. With the aid of a assistant who is holding open the vulva of the recipient cow, the technician will use a transfer gun to pass through the cervix. The top of the gun will deposit the embryo in the uterine horn, which contains the CL. For this immediate transfer, the embryo should be used within the first eight hours after the flush. If all goes well, the embryo will settle in the uterine wall and the transfer will be a success.

The other graded embryos will follow the same transfer procedure but they will be kept frozen in liquid nitrogen until the needed time arrives.

No matter which procedure of breeding is used, be it natural with bull, artificial insemination, or embryo transfer, the most important part is the genetic qualities of the donor and the bull The second factor is time. If this a full-time commercial cattle operation or a small one with the operator having an outside time consuming job, the ET procedure is not really practical because it is extremely time consuming. Unless there is a full-time technician who is willing and able to primarily work around the clock, this is not for the average cattle producer. Plus, it is extremely expensive. In a report printed by the University of Arkansas, minimum cost of a pregnancy by embryo transfer is $250. There may be additional charges of $400 to $500 to cover feed, housing and general caring of the recipient cow from the beginning of the process to the selling of the offspring. Another add on is the cost of the semen which may be anywhere from $45 to $300. The question here might and should probably be, "What is your goal and what is your market?" If the owner is hoping to produce and sell high-priced pure-bred animals, then go for it, but it all comes down to the first question, "What is your goal?"

For Eagles Nest Ranch, the goal as stated before is the raising of F1 heifers to be sold to commercial, not pure bred, breeders as replacements for their herd. When needing pure bred Angus replacements cows for the Eagles Nest Ranch, the AI procedure is used. Semen collected from genetically selected Angus bulls living on the ranch, or collected semen purchased from a bull that fits the program will be used. When the calf is born, if a female, she will join the herd and will be impregnated so as to give birth when she is two years of age. If a male with great qualities, he may be sold as a bull to other producers but more than likely, he will be castrated at two months of age, and as a steer will go to a feedlot.

I had so much to learn but I have succeeded to the point of understanding all the procedures. Breeding all comes down to starting out with the correct animals and appropriate procedures to achieve your finial goal.

Cow number 69, Casper, was involved in a surprising mix up but found a home at Eagles Nest Ranch.

On the lighter side of this chapter—Art and Greg, with the aid of a terrific technician (ET) produced a beautiful red and white Hereford bull. But here is the funny part. Greg had his own herd of Angus cows in Nebraska and we had ours in Colorado. Greg had an embryo transfer implanted in a black Angus cow with the ear tag number of 69. In the spring when Art went to Nebraska to bring our cows back to Colorado, he also had a black Angus cow with the number of 69. Thinking all was well, Art brought his load home. When cow #69 started the birthing procedure, two white hooves appeared. "What is the world is happening?" Angus calves should not have white hooves, grey, yes, but not white. As the calf continued the birthing process, it became evident, something was wrong. Oh! The Hereford calf was fine but Art was totally surprised that a purebred Hereford was birthed by a purebred Angus cow. The mix-up was when Greg's #69 got put in the trailer and our #69 remained in Nebraska. The black white-faced calf, born in Nebraska eventually came to Eagles Nest Ranch joining the rest of the herd. The red bull calf was eventually named "Casper" by two young boys who were visiting the ranch when he was born. Over the years Casper aided in the production of many AngusXHereford calves so once again, all's well that ends well!

DEERE JOHN

Tractor

One day while picking up trash in the pasture, I realized I had mentioned the tractor in various chapters but had never told a story about it. It wasn't until I was actually knocked down by the bucket on the front of the tractor that I realized how important it is in the overall operation of the ranch.

The definition of a tractor in 1900 was it was a "steam engine." That certainly would not be suitable in our situation. A tractor is a means of transportation and by itself, is just that. Today the tractor is powered by a diesel engine, not only replacing the steam engine but also a team of horses or mules. What makes the machine the work horse it is, are the attachments placed either on the front or rear of the tractor. The attachments required on the ranch are quite different than those of farmers who plant crops.

After the first five years ranching, fifty-pound small hay bales were becoming increasingly hard to find. Art decided a tractor was needed. Not just any tractor, but one that could be equipped to unroll the big round bales of hay that were being harvested by various farmers, especially the ones providing hay for Eagles Nest Ranch. Also, as we were becoming a bit older and much wiser, there certainly was a need for such a vehicle. So a search was begun and ended when Art found a one year old John Deere four wheel drive 5500 in Holdrege, Nebraska, twenty miles from his home town.

Bucket and Grapple Hooks

This John Deere tractor, green with its yellow buck painted on the side, was purchased for use on our ranch. It was equipped with a bucket and grapple hooks.

For me, a bucket was a large pail and I certainly did not know what a grapple hook was. The steel bucket is about seven feet across from one side to the other, attached to the front of the tractor by heavy rods to a hydraulic lift mechanism. The grapple hook, also made of steel, consists of four curved prongs which may be lowered over

"Smoke" Glinnsman delivering the first of four loads of hay that are needed each year at Eagles Nest Ranch. The hay will be unloaded and stacked by using the grapple hook on the tractor.

the bucket, thereby holding various objects in place. On the ranch, the big bale of hay is settled into the bucket and held in place by the grapple hooks. Many days, I would ride along on the tractor, standing on a step beside Art, hopping on and off to open gates as he went from one pasture to another to feed the herd. But one day he said to me, "You will need to help so we can move some panels from one pasture to another." My response was, "Oh, my gosh!" I had absolutely no knowledge as to the workings of the tractor or its attachments. But not wanting to be unhelpful, I positioned myself in the tractor's seat. Listening carefully to his instructions, I was shown which lever did what to the bucket or the grapple hook. Patience was definitely required by Art as I struggled to move the bucket as well as the grapple hook precisely as ordered to complete the project at hand. "Oops" was heard quite often but by days end, I had learned a new lesson and had actually driven the tractor. (Add "grapple hook" to my vocabulary.) The bucket and grapple hook remain on the tractor most of the time as they are the most used attachments and their usage are written about in various situations. During the summer months, the bucket and grapple hook are removed unless they are needed for "clean up" operations of all kinds.

Bucket and grappling hook used for moving big bales of hay.

Hay Bale Unrollller

The next important attachment is the "hay bale unroller" attached by steel tubes to the rear of the tractor. These hooks are located on a bar stretching across the rear of the

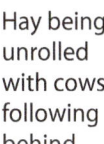

Hay being unrolled with cows following behind.

tractor with arms protruding outward ending with round steel disks that have a steel hook facing inward. When a hay bale is to be removed from the hay stack, the tractor will back up, positioning itself so that when the bar is raised by a lever on the tractor, the arms will enter the bale with the hooks from either side positioned tightly in the middle of the bale. The tractor is driven into the pasture and the bale lowered to the ground. It is driven slowly forward as the hay is rolled flatly onto the pasture. This procedure allows the cows to spread out while eating and without having to take turns at a hay feeder ring. When there are calves with their mothers, it is not unusual to see the calves laying in the middle of unrolled hay with mothers eating around or over them. If there is a pile of hay anywhere in the pastures, the calves will find it and use it as their bed.

Manure Spreader

Another use for the bucket is when the corrals need to be cleared of manure. The bucket will be lowered to the ground so that it acts as a scoop. When it is filled, it will be tipped up, driven by the tractor to a "manure spreader" attached to another tractor, or in Art's case, connected to the Gator. Here again was another new term for me, not necessarily the word "manure" but the fact that there is a spreader designed specifically for spreading manure. When the spreader is full, it is driven to a pasture and with a flip of a lever, manure will fly forth over the field. Hopefully, with

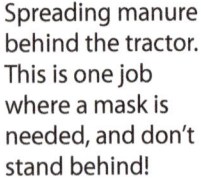
Spreading manure behind the tractor. This is one job where a mask is needed, and don't stand behind!

aid from rain, the manure will help replenish grass growing in the pasture. We can only hope! A piece of advice: wear a mask and definitely DO NOT STAND BEHIND THE SPREADER!!! The dry manure is like a fine dust when being applied to the ground and to a human, it would be comparable to being caught in a dust storm.

Bush Hog

"Bush Hog" was definitely a new term for me and it did create quite a response from my family. "Is a 'Bush Hog' a new breed of hogs?" We're cattle people and certainly not equipped to raise hogs. Growing up in Iowa and living in Indiana for all those years, "pigs" as I knew them, were not an unidentified object. I had heard Greg speaking about different breeds of hogs as he had judged them with the Pur-

Pasture mower known as the "Bush Hog."

due Judging team, so my questions were not really uncalled for. What a shock I had when the guys stopped laughing and told me the "bush hog" was a piece of equipment that would make cutting weeds in the pastures much easier and faster. Ok, but why is it called a "Bush Hog?" On this I definitely needed to do some research!

The implement called a "Bush Hog" is simply a five-foot-wide rotary cutter mounted to the rear of a tractor and is similar to one under the familiar riding lawn mower. It was originally designed with a three-point lift, a stump jumper and swinging blades that could fold back if they hit heavy objects, such as rocks. Before this invention farmers would have to rely on manual labor. At one time, while Greg was working on a farm in Indiana, he would ride in a bucket on the front of the tractor looking for rocks as the tractor traversed the fields in preparation for the seasons planting of seeds. Not a fun job, and certainly not an easy on the body ride, but necessary and very time consuming.

According to "Bush Hog. com", the name came after a man watching the 1951 demonstration of the implement in Selma, Alabama, said, "That thing eats bushes like a hog." Since I had never seen a hog eating bushes, I cannot verify the truth of the statement but it does make a good story!

On our ranch the "Bush Hog" is used to mow a field where there is a large outcropping of weeds. In doing so, the tops of the weeds will be cut off, preventing the seeds from maturing. As a result, the cattle will be more likely to graze the forage surrounding the unpalatable plant. This implement will also be used to cut the grass around the farmstead and the roadside outside the perimeter fence.

One thing for sure, there are no "live hogs" involved in this operation!

Sprayer

Unfortunately, weeds tend to grow in pastures. Some of them are the plants that produce the beautiful assortment of spring flowers but there are also those clas-

Sprayer to rid the pastures of noxious weeds.

sified as noxious (harmful) weeds. (Another new term for me) There are many varieties of these weeds but two common to Eagles Nest Ranch are Canada thistle and Common mullein. Both are considered aggressive plants and if not controlled, may overtake the valuable pasture land. The solution for this problem, is to spray. If there is only a small patch, spraying may be accomplished by using a small tank of a herbicide mixture placed in a tank in the back of the John Deere Gator and sprayed with a singular wand by the rancher as he/she drives around the pastures. However, if there is much acreage, a large tank will be attached to the rear of the tractor. This tank has two booms which fold up when not in use, but when operational, will open out like outstretched arms covered with individual sprayers which can cover a twenty-five-foot span. This tank hold approximately two hundred gallons of herbicide and is powered by the power take-off on the tractor. This involves many hours of labor but is better than violating the law since one is obligated by law to control designated noxious weeds.

Log Splitter

During the summer months when the cows are out on the pasture with their calves, there is a time when all the other projects that had been put aside, may now be undertaken. There is always fence repairing but that goes on continually. Now is the time to remove dead trees but only if there has been enough moisture so there is no fire danger. There are many trees on the ranch so this is a never-ending job. One of our friends, Dr. Robert Noyd, from the Air Force Academy, had cored one of the old Juniper trees and had gotten in as far as he could before hitting rotten wood. He determined that this tree was at least two hundred or more years old. In the early settlement of this region there was a saw mill about five miles south of the ranch so it may be presumed the ranch was even more densely populated with a variety of trees. It may also be presumed that many of the original trees were cut for lumber and sent to Denver on the narrow-gauge train to be used in building homes. Every year a number of the still standing trees are found dead due to age but others, not having a deep root system, have been blown down due to high winds. In either case, there are dead trees that need to be removed.

When the sun is shining, there is a cool breeze and the soil is moist, it is a good day to cut trees. Art gets his saw, oil, gloves, safety glasses and determination that today is the day! A utility trailer is hooked to the truck and the log splitter (another attachment) is mounted on the tractor. PAUL BUNYAN and spouse (me) head to the woods. Once a tree is cut and lowered to the ground, the branches are removed, cut into fireplace size logs, and stacked or put in the trailer.

When the cutting of the trunk is begun, so is the work of the log splitter. The log is put on an I beam that has a cutter bar on one end. A hydraulic cylinder with a plate on the other end pushes the log to the cutting bar. My job is to pull the handle to activate the hydraulic cylinder and by all means, I must keep my hands out of the way. "Oh, my gosh!" Just another learning event! Not only had I never seen such an outfit, I certainly did not know how one worked. I quickly learned as there was work to be done. When the splitting is finished, all the logs are loaded into the trailer, the excess trash is cleaned up and off we go to unload this high pile of wood.

Unloading should be the easy part of this project. WRONG! The trailer will be parked about one hundred feet from the already established wood stack. It is impossible to get any closer because of large rocks and a deck connected to the house that must be navigated. "Watch your head" is heard quite often. Not being quitters, we go about the task of unloading the wood. This is achieved by taking the logs from the trailer, putting them into a wheelbarrow and pushing it down a slight incline to where the wood is being stacked. Of course, I could stand by the trailer and just throw the logs down the hill, but if one should land wrong, Art would not be a "Happy Camper" so the wheelbarrow is returned, reloaded and the procedure continues.

The best part of this whole project is during the winter when at least one of the three fireplaces located in the house is fired up, this wood produces a nice warm feeling throughout the whole room.

In addition to the ponderosa pines and junipers, there are various bushes such as mountain mahogany, snowberry, skunk bush and choke cherry, all of which provide food for the deer. I planted a couple of "Fire Bushes" hoping to get some red color in the fall but, lo and behold, the deer got to them, stripped them clean and made it impossible for the bushes to survive. So much for color! If we want color, we may look across the road to view the yellow leaves on the Cottonwood trees growing along the creek bed or better yet, we can drive to the mountains and enjoy the gold of the Aspen trees.

Tourist Attraction

The tractor plays an important part on the ranch, not only as a farm implement but it serves as a tourist attraction, especially for little boys. There have been many occasions when little boys around three or four years of age will visit the ranch. Quite often they will be seen standing by the tractor, just looking at this huge vehicle with wheels much higher than they are tall. "Whatever are they thinking?" but when asked if they would like to "hop on" the smile on their faces stretch from ear to ear. Sitting high on the yellow seat of the green John Deere, posing for a photo-op by parents/grandparents, one arm stretches out to the steering wheel. It is suddenly joined by the second arm and soon hands are clutching the wheel, all the time, making a whirring sound, as if they are driving. The smile has gone as far across the face as it can, but now even the eyes are sparkling. What a wonderful experience these young boys will share with their friends.

I have learned one thing for sure. When men of all ages who were raised on a farm get together, they will always remember the first tractor they drove, the make, model, color, and absolutely every fine detail. Why is it these same men cannot remember what they needed from the grocery or any other store? So it is!!!

Hay Rides

Another important job for the tractor, but not an everyday function, is that of pulling the old wooden wagon filled with hay and visitors to the ranch, especially when there are more than just a few. Who gains the most from this adventure is open to debate but it is a time of "oohs" and "aahs" as the cows gather around the wagon. The cows know that visitors mean "treats" as cubes are hand fed to the cows with their tongues sticking out and always ready to accept more.

One memorable hay ride was when a group of retired ELANCO employees and former co-workers of Art were visiting the ranch. Jack McAskill had a large two-wheeled wagon which would accommodate a large group of people and with the Ford 550 flatbed also filled to capacity, they headed out to the pasture. All of a sudden, the trailer being pulled by Jack's tractor would not move. One of the back wheels had completely departed from the trailer leaving the trailer in a precarious situation. Fortunately, not a single person slid off. All were carefully removed. Some were loaded on the flatbed truck while others decided it was much safer walking the mile back to the barn where lunch was waiting. The trailer remained in the field for a couple more days before being repaired. Everyone had a good time. The event still makes for a great memory.

We are more than willing to share their ranch with city folk and what fun it is when they all reschedule a visit.

Visitors to the ranch enjoy a hay ride
with cows coming to visit for treats.

STEWARDS OF THE LAND

Farmers and ranchers are undoubtably the best stewards of the grazing land and its natural resources. They have to be as their livelihood depends on it. Every rock, not pebbles, but rocks the size of two fists or larger take up space that would otherwise be used for growing crops or grassland for grazing cattle.

From conversations with neighbors and other ranchers we often heard the terms "Cross fencing" and "Rotational grazing." These were both new terms in our vocabulary but ones we certainly wanted to look into. Wanting to become good stewards of our land, we certainly wanted to do the cross fencing and rotational grazing but to do so, we needed professional help to develop a workable plan. For this, we turned to the United States Department of Agriculture Soils and Conservation Service.

Their experts, very willing to help us, came to the ranch equipped with a topographic map and cameras. They walked the entire ranch, with the exception of the area south of the barn which had already been divided into two operational sections classified as "winter pasture." Notes were made concerning the variety of natural grasses, plants, wild flowers, location of trees and the outcropping of rocks. Additionally, they noted the many areas of flat land and draws covered with really good grass suitable for the grazing of cattle.

From these observations, a map dividing the pasture into four parts with equal grazing potential was drawn up. Consideration was also given to the amount of rainfall as this drought prone region receives only about fourteen inches of moisture a year. We were told that the plan for rotational grazing by using the existing well in the center of the four sections, the ranch would support sixty-two cow/calf pairs from May to October. Now, with map in hand, wood stakes and hammer in a bucket in the back of the golf cart, we began to lay out the future cross fencing.

Cross Fencing

The first step was to build a corral fence around the water tank in the center of the four sections. Each section has a gate from the pastures and when open the cattle are free to go into the corral for water supplied by the windmill which fills the huge water tank. Because all other gates remain closed, the cattle must return to their original pasture and this is where the "rotational grazing" comes into being.

When the project was completed, we had constructed a total of eight and one half miles of fencing. When we were doing this, we would get up early in the morning, go out with fencing gear and work until noon. About three in the afternoon, we would go back out and work until just before dark. This way, we would avoid the heat of the day but dinner would be very late, if at all!

Corral fence around the water tank and windmill..

Rotation Grazing

Now Art and I were ready to implement "rotational grazing." Understanding the digestive system of cows/ruminants made it easier for me to appreciate the importance of cattle to the world food supply and ecosystem. Basically, the cows eat the grass and other plants in the pastures. Their digestive system allows them to thrive on forage and also aids in seed germination and fertilization for new growth which aids in the stabilization of the ground, preventing erosion of the soil according to an article I read by Nicolette Hahn Niman, of the *Wall Street Journal*.

We did not know the importance of the cows in the overall scheme of nature. We were doing rotational grazing so the grass would improve allowing us to enlarge our herd. Where the ranch is located the Soil Conservation Service say it takes twenty acres of pasture for each pair (cow and calf) due to the low rainfall in this area. Rotational grazing reduces the acreage needed for each cow/calf pair from twenty down to fourteen.

Rotation changes each year. On Eagles Nest Ranch, there are four sections of summer pasture. The first year the cattle graze the pasture in the southwest section. After a period of about six weeks, depending on moisture and availability of grass, the cows were moved to the northwest. Six weeks later to the northeast and ending in the southeast pasture. This procedure forces them to "clean up their plates" before moving to the next section. The following year, the procedure will begin with cows in the northwest pasture through to the southwest. It is important for each section to rest during the early spring growth at least one of every four years. With our system, each pasture will rest three out of every four years.

It always seems to me that the animals know when they will be moved to a new section where they will have their "dessert." The cows and calves watch us as we drive through the pasture in the white truck, with someone sitting on the back of the flatbed holding a bag of cubes (treats for cows). The truck driver stops, opens the gate and then drives into the new pasture, all the time, honking the horn. The truck is followed by the John Deere Gator at a distance behind the cows with the driver yelling out "Go, go, go." It does not take the cows long to realize they are going to new greener pastures and before long, they run past the truck, fanning out in all directions, with heads down and mouths chomping away on new grass. Before settling down to serious grazing, they go exploring around the whole pasture as if looking for their own very special "restaurant." They especially like the blossoms on the yucca plants if available, it is usually their first choice.

Practicing "rotational grazing" results in "well managed grazing land." We wonder why more ranchers are not following this procedure. Looking back, our conservation began before we were living on the ranch. I had gone to Denver to meet with the builders of our house and while there I was asked to plant some grass where fill dirt for the driveway had been removed. I quickly learned that regular grass seed was not an option but the special "native grass" seed from the Soil Conservation Service was required. I borrowed a hand held seed thrower from a friend and set out to do the job. All of a sudden I noticed clouds building and the temperature was falling, a clear sign a storm was approaching. So, instead of using the seeder I stood down wind and started hand sowing the seed. What a glorious sight it was a couple of months later when there was green grass heartily growing in the distressed area.

Mineral Feeders supply mineral supplements required for enumerable steps in animal metabolism.

Mineral Feeders

The placement of mineral feeders in the pastures is an important part of conservation. Mineral supplements supply the salt as well as major minerals, phosphorus, calcium, magnesium for growth and lactation as well as trace minerals required for enumerable steps in animal metabolism. The feeders are put in the pastures during the periods of rotation but to save the grass, they are relocated periodically. This way the grass surrounding the feeders will not be eaten down beyond repair or regrowth. It also forces the cattle to use all parts of the pasture as they are quite fond of the minerals.

It is amazing how quickly the calves take to the feeder. Apparently after watching their moms stick their heads in the feeder, the calves, at an early stage, will follow suit. It is fun watching the calves lick their faces after having eaten the minerals. It is sort of like a child after tasting ice cream for the first time.

Cows drinking from the water tank in the center of four pasture section.

Water and Conservation

"Water, water everywhere but not a drop to drink" is an often-quoted line from The Ancient Mariner. In Colorado is could be "no water anywhere and the animals need a drink." It really isn't that bad but water is a precious resource.

On the ranch there are three wells, two for the land and one for the house. The well at the barn serves not only the large water tank during the warm months but also the electrically heated water tanks during the winter. These are used by the cows/calves in the winter pastures and by the cows in the southeast and southwest pastures during the summer rotation. These cows also have access to the well in the center of the four pastures during the summer. Water is supplied to the northwest and northeast pastures from the center tank as well as from an additional tank located between the northwest and northeast pastures which receives overflow water through an underground pipe draining down forty feet in elevation. There is never a time when all water tanks will be in operation at the same time. It all depends on which pasture is being grazed and which gates are open to the various tanks. The solar powered well in the north may be turned off if both water tanks are full and it is turned off during the winter months.

One time we were asked to work with the U.S. Soil Conservation Service in putting three or four wire ladders inside the water tanks so the birds could climb out of the water. This project went on for five years. Art claims he saw some using the ladders to escape. I did not spend my time sitting by a water tank watching for birds so saw very few birds even going to the large tank. They prefer to sit on the ledges of the smaller individual water tanks in the corrals. Every now and then a calf will find themselves in the larger tank, but it takes a human with waders on to rescue this creature!

While we are primarily concerned about the importance of pasture grass for our animals, another conservation practice rarely brought up is that 75% of the pastures are free of cattle during the hatching period of birds.

Historical Conservation Water Stories

Kiowa Creek Flood

On May 30-31, 1935 there was a devastating flood, not only in Elbert but all along the Kiowa Creek. Prior to the flood, eastern Colorado had been in a terrible drought and was considered to be part of the "Dust Bowl." On May 30, at 9:30 A.M. the rain began. Not just rain but a deluge causing local basements to flood. It is written that "skies cleared forenoon, but rain resumed around noon" (James Jones) I look at the terrain on Eagles Nest Ranch and noticing the drop in elevation, I can easily imagine the rain water flowing quickly to join Kiowa Creek across the road. We have experienced flooding on the ranch but nothing as severe as the one in 1935. It was estimated that seventy buildings were damaged or worse, washed away in Elbert alone. A corner of the high school was damaged causing graduation exercises to be cancelled. The narrow-gauge railroad track was washed out and never rebuilt. The concrete base of the water tower for the trains steam engine remains on the east side of the main street in Elbert. Twenty-four inches of rain fell in a period of twelve hours, leaving the whole town in a total disaster. Scenes of Elbert after the flood show what appears to be piles upon piles of mud on the streets with debris absolutely everywhere. I wish I could have interviewed flood survivors to hear what would surely have been amazing stories but by now, there are none around. The ones that are, were too young to remember that day so I must rely on published accounts. Some of the original buildings remain and are operational while others are empty with tales to tell.

Before the flood, Elbert had been considered a summer retreat for Denverites as it was at a higher elevation and much cooler in the summer months. It was served by the narrow-gauge railroad making transportation from Denver, Colorado Springs and even Pueblo convenient. Main street was home to a hotel, a general store, a post office, a livery stable and many cottages. There was also a saloon and two churches. The Presbyterian Church was, and still is, located on a high hill so was quite possibly a refuge for residents fleeing the rising flood water.

As a result of this flood, in 1951, a Kiowa Creek Flood Control committee was formed. They met with the House of Representatives Subcommittee on soil conservation and flood control of the committee on Agriculture in Colby, Kansas. Speaking to the committee was Dewey Carnahan, owner of the oldest ranch in Elbert County.

> "We've come quite a way from Colorado in order to be at this meeting, even though we understand that your meeting is primarily concerned with Kansas, we have a problem that individual people cannot reach and a problem that the army engineers and bureau of reclamation people cannot reach. What we need, we feel, is flood retardation dams which Congressman Paige expressed very well. Because of the terrific cloud bursts, we need a large agency or at least the authority to empower some existing agency to build flood control dams. The amount of silt that comes off the steep drainage is astounding."

This resulted in the building of sixty-three check dams in the Kiowa Creek valley which is 123 miles in length. The west Kiowa Creek starts at an elevation of 7,540 feet in El Paso County, flowing north through Elbert, where it joins East Kiowa Creek, which starts at the same elevation but at a different location also in El Paso County. The creek rises in the highland of Colorado Piedmont and is suspect to an occasional flood. It is considered an intermittent creek which means there is not always water flowing, or in some cases, it could be flowing but not observed on the surface. Kiowa Creek flows north and joins the South Platte River which flows into Missouri River and then into the Mississippi River ending in the Gulf of Mexico.

Check Dams

"Wikipedia" defines a check dam as "a small dam constructed across a swale, drainage ditch, or waterway to counteract erosion by reducing water flow velocity." The Eagles Nest Ranch has four earthen check dams situated in critical areas constructed from 1957 to 1962 by local contractors. All of the dams are maintained by the Kiowa Conservation District and are inspected annually. It is stated that without these dams, 2,500 – 3,000 acres of agricultural lands could be susceptible to extensive flooding.

Concrete structure that drains the water.

Eagles Nest Ranch experienced a flood in 2016. The ranch buildings were not affected but there was a large amount of water running through the draw toward the dam. The large check dam held the water back but water in the east pasture was gushing through the culverts like one would see watching water flow over a regular dam. What water that does not get though the check dam is left behind and will eventually soak into the ground. This time the water was about twelve feet deep and reached the top of the concrete drain structure built into the dam. The water ran full bore through a three-foot-wide culvert draining the dam. There was so much debris left behind as the neighbors upstream had piled wood in the flood plain. The wood washed down stream, tearing out three fences which were later repaired and parts replaced by stronger wire, hoping to prevent future fence damage. The close neighbor's drive was also damaged. The funny part of all of this was, the teenage son of the wood owner was sent over to retrieve all the logs. He came with a three-wheeler and picked up one piece at a time taking it one half mile back home and then returning to start the procedure all over again. It was going to take him forever so I suggested his father might come over with a truck to help. This never happened so we ended up with a few very large logs in the pasture which remained flooded for almost a year and a half before completely drying up. If we had been younger, we might have gone ice skating in the winter as it was a convenient spot with a warming house (barn) within walking distance. All this water was not all bad as it provided a landing place for ducks, geese or heron giving ranchers the thrill of watching the birds. Isn't nature wonderful?

Check damn with pasture filled with water.

Flood water flowing through culvert.

Kiowa Creek Flood of 1965

"Rain and floods are the conversation of the day" as reported in the June 17th issue of the Elbert County News. The flood was a result of a tornado that had hit Palmer Lake, a community southwest of Elbert. Tornado warnings had been issued for Castle Rock but the "wind blew the threatening clouds east into the Elbert/Kiowa area where the skies dumped a deluge in the Kiowa Creek, East Bijou Creek and various gulches, creeks enroute north about 6:00 p.m." Another article states that "East Kiowa Creek rose and met West Kiowa Creek just a rollin' into Elbert and Kiowa. The Elbert-Kiowa area was darkened and socked in by deep fog and flooded about 6:30 p.m. or so."

Elbert received about four inches of rain in a two-to-three-hour period of time. The amount of rain was not really what caused the flood. I spoke with Kay Royston who stated, "It had been a relative dry year until April and May when we received a lot of snow and rain. The ground was saturated, causing runoff, filling the creeks to overflowing. It was so bad that even some of the smaller check dams were wiped out by water flowing over the spillways." The construction of the check dams had been completed in the early 1960s and what a blessing that proved to be. Without them, while there was considerable damage with bridges being washed out, fences completely destroyed, gravel roads made impossible to use, conditions would have been MUCH, MUCH worse. If the dams had not been doing a TERRIFIC job of holding back the rushing water as it moved downstream to join the South Platte River, it would be hard to say how much fertile land would have been completely washed away or covered with silt rendering it non-productive.

No lives were lost in Elbert but it was reported that "A number of cattle drowned." One rancher "lost a valuable Hereford bull" while another lost "a three-thousand-dollar Black Angus bull."

The Importance of Conservation

In a region having only fourteen inches of moisture in a year, each and every snow flake and drop of rain is an important resource for ranchers. The moisture supplies nutrients for growth of pasture grass which enables the ranchers to raise beef. The facts are "a billion of the world's poorest population depend on livestock" for dinner. In an article "Defending Beef: The Case for Sustainable Meat Production" by Nicolette Hahn Niman, Ms. Niman says, "As we consider the long-term prospects for feeding the human race, cattle will rightly remain an essential element!" "BEEF IS WHAT'S FOR DINNER" is a sign often seen in TV advertisements. ONLY CATTLE, SHEEP AND GOATS CAN CONVERT THE WORLDS FORAGE (GRASS) INTO HUMAN FOOD (MEAT AND MILK).

Art. Greg and myself will continue all conservation practices which aid in sustainable production of F1 calves whose offspring will supply the beef needed to feed "the human race." (Niman) We are proud to say that Eagles Nest Ranch was recognized by the Kiowa Soil Conservation District as Conservationist of the Year in 1998.

DON'T LIKE THE WEATHER?, WAIT FIVE MINUTES

As a child or even as an adult, did you ever lay flat on your back on the soft green grass or sit in a lounge chair just looking at the sky and the movement of the clouds? Of course, you did. Everyone has and how many times would you say "I see a face in that cloud" or "Is that a duck or chicken?" The sky over Eagles Nest Ranch, because of the proximity to the mountains, provides many spectacular views of all sorts of cloud formations.

Watching the storm clouds from a high point on Eagles Nest Ranch.

There are the "storm across the meadows" clouds sung about by John Denver. Art and I can go to a high point of the ranch, where we have a 360 degree look at the sky and the formation of storm clouds. The sky may have virga in one area showing grey rain clouds with hanging thin clouds looking like a veil, with no rain or precipitation reaching the ground. Off in another direction is a column of dark cumulus clouds, producing quite a rain shower. There could also be sections of white coming out of the cloud, indicating the possibility of hail or snow depending on the temperature and time of the year. Another view could be the bright sun producing a rainbow or even a double one with colors covering the sky with the pot of gold at either end.

Virga clouds have trails of precipitation that fall but evaporate before it reaches the ground.

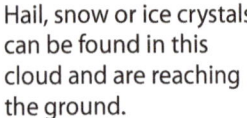

Hail, snow or ice crystals can be found in this cloud and are reaching the ground.

Lenticular clouds are often seen at the ranch caused by wind currents over the mountains.

There are many different cloud formations but ones seen quite often are lenticular clouds. They are saucer shaped, like the lens of the human eye and are caused by the rising and falling wind currents coming over the mountains. Sometimes they get stacked one on top of the other, looking like a stack of pancakes. This formation, usually only seen in close proximity to the mountains, was of great interest when first observed by me. Sighting lenticular clouds is a good indication of a weather change as they are created by strong western winds coming across and sweeping down the eastern side of the Rockies.

Trail clouds looks like a cork screw are found toward the southwest of a thunder storm.

Wave cloud take on the shape of an apostrophe and hint at turbulence in the sky.

There is another interesting shaped cloud that to me looks like a cork screw. It is wide at the beginning with what appears to be rings that gradually get narrower toward the end. Scientifically, it is called a Trail cloud and is found toward the southwest of a thunder storm.

One day a series of clouds shaped like apostrophes (") were seen close to the foothills. Being extremely curious, I found they are called "Wave clouds." According to Earthsky.org., this is a special kind of cloud that resemble breaking ocean waves, formed when two different layers of air are moving at different speeds with the upper layer moving at the higher speed. They often form on windy days and are good indicators of atmospheric instability causing turbulence for aircraft. This is an interesting sight to see and now that I know more about it, I am more than happy to observe it from the ground and not from the air.

Then there are always the tornado clouds. The ones everyone needs to be concerned about and possibly take immediate precautionary measures. A tornado is defined as rotating columns of air and since air is invisible, a person must rely on the reporting of weather personnel. Living in Indiana for thirty-one years makes me always sit up and take notice when a "Tornado Alert Warning" is issued. I was at the Post Office in Elbert one nice clear day when I saw people standing in the middle of the street looking toward a high hill behind a row of houses. I wondered what they were looking at so, being nosey, I also took a look. There was a huge white cloud and I immediately thought of a tornado. I hurried home, drove down the drive, honking the car horn, hoping to alert Art that a storm was approaching. When I found Art, I said, "Get in the car. There is a tornado and we need to get to the house and shelter." Being very calm, Art responded, "I've got to close the barn door." For anyone who has observed tornado destruction, you know that a barn can be destroyed with or without the doors being closed. We did go to the house and watched the tornado go south of the ranch by about five miles, leaving some destruction but nothing serious. Tornado warnings should not be taken lightly, but it is human nature to watch, especially when tornadoes are not as common in Colorado as they are in the "Tornado Alley" of the mid-west.

It is not uncommon for the thunderstorms to form in the afternoon on the front range of the Rockies. These storms are known as "Convective" storms and form

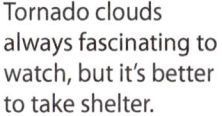
Tornado clouds always fascinating to watch, but it's better to take shelter.

because the heating of the ground which then heats the air producing columns of air called "thermals." As the air rises it is cooled and cannot hold as much water vapor so clouds begin to form. According to Mike Nelson in The Colorado Weather Book, as the clouds grow, moisture condenses into water drops and eventually, these heavy drops become rain and fall to the earth. It seems as if these storms form east of the foothills of the Rocky Mountains and build up as they pass over the

Eagles Nest Ranch. By nightfall they are far out to the east reaching the Kansas and Nebraska borders. We can look eastward observing the building severe storm with clouds filled with lightning and rain. It is always a sight to behold but as ranchers, we were wishing we had been on the receiving part of the rain.

Convective clouds formed during thunderstorms common in the afternoon at Eagles Nest.

Cows as Weather Watchers

Neither Art nor I will ever be professional weather reporters but it is interesting to speculate on what we might learn if we could talk to the cows. So many times, I wished I could read the cows and their reaction to forth coming storms. In the summer months when there is the possibility and probability of afternoon storm, it seems that about an hour before the storm, the cows will call for their calves. After grouping together, they will all move to low places in the pasture. Now this is not a proven scientific fact but it does happen frequently and always in the same manner. Seems like more than a coincidence!

The cows seem to have a schedule determined by the weather. When the cool days of spring have arrived, the animals will congregate in the corral that is covered with dark dirt and will be absorbing the warm sunlight. They arrive about ten o'clock in the morning, have their turn at the water tank, and then proceed to lay around until about three o'clock. At this time, they slowly walk to the pasture where they start their afternoon of grazing. During the summer, the cows will predict the hot temperature for the day early in the morning. It is not unusual to see them gathered under the trees, as if they know for sure it is going to be really hot. They leave their spot to get water but quickly return to the shade. In winter, in case of a blizzard, the cows put their butts to the wind and walk ahead of the snow. Many years ago, thousands of cattle in south eastern Colorado died as a result of a blizzard. The snow was so deep the cows walked over fences, falling into gullies on top of others and eventually suffocating. It was a terrible disaster and was quite news worthy. Hopefully, it will never be repeated. This also explains why we built two snow shelters on the Eagle Nest ranch to shield the cows from blowing snow.

There was one night during the second year of calving when I was alone at the ranch while Art was bringing cows home from Nebraska. The day had been a beautiful Colorado day with the night came a "First Alert Action." Looking back on this experience, I should have watched the cows a bit closer. Blizzard conditions were predicted, and since I had heard this alarm before, I decided to wait to see if, in fact, it was to be a reality. About 8:30 that evening, it began to snow. The wind was not violent but not calm either. I, being a mother, decided since there were only seven new calves in the corral, they really needed to be brought into the barn along with their mothers. Six pens were clean so new straw was spread, gates were rearranged, making room for all seven. The six pens already had automatic watering facilities so I only needed to put a tub of hay in each pen. That accomplished, the make-shift pen needed a tub of water and hay. That done, I tried moving this small herd. Not a single cow or calf wanted to be moved. Here's where I should have been listening. But "No," I called my neighbor Al Colyer for help. He said he was already for bed but would be glad to come and help. Not wanting to wait, I tried one more time to move the animals. This time I was successful, except for one calf who came in with the assistence of Al. OK. Everyone was in and settled. The seventh pen was a success. So, all was well. I was pleased with my efforts when all of a sudden there was a butting on the barn door. The one and only bull had been left outside and he must have felt deserted. So, once again, being a mother, always a mother, another gate was moved, the barn door opened and the bull joined the party! "Oh, my gosh" was all Art could say when he returned the next day. The storm really hadn't been that bad and in reality, the cows and calves had been quite safe in the corral. Just another lesson for me to learn!

Weather Changes Demand Clothes Changes

Another aspect of weather watching involves how many times a day there will be a change of clothes. For those of you who live in Colorado, the answer could be, "many times." During the summer months, morning will find me in a shirt, sweatshirt and jeans. By noon, the attire is changed to only the shirt and maybe a pair of shorts. Of course, this all depends on the project for the day. By five o'clock, the jeans are once again partnered with the sweatshirt. A jacket will be close by to be worn once the sun sets.

Springtime on the ranch is a whole different story as my attire depends wholly on what is happening out in the field. Since spring time is calving time, the day begins with the jeans, shirt and sweatshirt. But wait! It is staring to snow and there are pregnant cows that may need attending. Looking through the binoculars, there is cow off by herself by the check dam. "Quick, let's see if we can bring her into the shed or barn so she will be out of the weather." The optimum word here is "Quick." There is no time to waste - no boots and no coveralls or flannel lined jeans. Just grab the closest warm coat, stocking cap and of course, warm gloves. After successfully attending to the cow, it means a change of clothes as who wants to sit around in wet jeans, not to mention, the pant legs possibly being covered with mud or whatever! The gloves are insulated, perfect for winter days but since snow is extremely wet, the gloves also need to be changed. The cap is hung up so it will dry and a pair of dry gloves is put on stand by for the next emergency.

This does not even consider if one has changed from jeans, etc. to pajamas. Since cows do not deliver babies on human clock time, another "Quick" is bound to occur before the night is over. This means back to jeans, coveralls and warm coats. Are you getting the picture? Thank goodness for washers and dryers!

Snow Storms

For those of you living in the "snow belt," have you ever told your children "When I was growing up, I had to walk to school through snow up to my knees." Of course, you did not say how old you were or that your knees were closer to the ground. Undoubtably their comeback was "Yeah, yeah, and it was up hill both ways."

Snow storms are quite common in Colorado with most occurring from late November through late April and early May. The more snow the better for the ski areas as skiers mean money for the resorts. But most importantly, it provides much needed water for all the reservoirs and especially for all the ranches in Colorado. It means more moisture for summer grass.

Snow for skiers is great but for ranchers it is an entirely different situation. When the ground is covered, it is understood that the ranchers must provide hay for feed but even more important than the feeding is the close watching of pregnant cows making sure the cow/calves are all safe after birth. Also, drastic changes in the weather, especially a change from real cold to really warm could cause respiratory illnesses, such as pneumonia which is the number one health challenge for cattle.

In September of 1993 we were caught off guard when the first snow of the season appeared. We were awakened by horizontal snow hitting the window of the house in the middle of the night. Like firemen having their gear readily available, so did we. The uniform of the day was the heaviest and warmest clothes which were hanging on hooks by the back door. Boots and of course, the always ready GLOVES were quickly gathered up as the sleepy-eyed ranchers headed for the "good ole red pickup." The cross fencing had not been accomplished so the cows were somewhere out in the wide-open pasture. Art asked me "How are we going to get the cows down to the winter pasture?" My simple answer was, "We'll start honking the horn as we go down the drive." The cows knew that the honking of the horn meant they might get "treats." We got to the barn and were waiting but no cows were appearing. I was getting very anxious so decided to go back up to the house and honk the horn

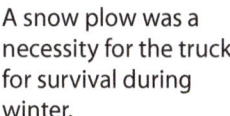

A snow plow was a necessity for the truck for survival during winter.

Snow storm of 1997 left Elbert County under sixteen inches of snow with drifts twelve feet deep.

again. I did this, but also had the truck window open. All of a sudden, there was a "Moo" coming from quite a distance. I went back to join Art and said, "The cows will be here soon." It was just a matter of minutes before some of the cows came down the drive and others came around the north side of the barn. They were successfully put in the winter pasture and yes, the cows did get some treats. We spent the rest of the night sleeping in the barn.

It was after that night that we quickly realized a new plan of attack was needed. First, a snow plow was needed for the truck. Secondly, cupboards in the barn should be filled with non-perishable food. Added to that was a purchase of a small freezer to be filled with hamburger or beef cuts to be used in soup on snowy days. Also needed were snow tires for the truck - Most Important!

When all these conditions were met, we were sure we could handle any storm but that proved not to be quite the case. On October 25, 1997 a snow storm hit Elbert County. The Elbert County News reported in the October 30th issues that Elbert had received sixteen inches of snow. The forty mile an hour wind produced drifts from five to twelve feet deep. The wind chill was a minus twenty below. Snow had been predicted so the pickup was loaded with hay and parked heading down from the house to the barn just in case it was needed. Boy was it needed! Dressed in the uniform of warm clothes, boots, hats and GLOVES, we took off for the barn. All was going well until Art turned the wheel, thinking he had reached the turn in the road taking us down the hill. He hit a huge rock, that had been completely covered by snow. I rose up from the seat and hit my head hard on the ceiling of the cab. The truck was STUCK! There was absolutely no way to maneuver out of the drift. The only thing the we could do was to get out of the truck and walk through the blizzard to the barn.

The decision was made to leave the cows in the pasture with trees where there would be some protection. After receiving forty-five inches of snow and not knowing where the cows were, it was impossible for the cows to get grass or to be fed hay for three to four days. When calving was over, we realized we had lost five calves due to miscarriages of the cows. This was due to the eating of pine needles by the pregnant cows. A lot of research has gone into this problem, but the only solution to the problem is to keep the cows out of the pine trees when the pastures are covered with snow.

As for us two legged creatures, it took us three days before we could get back to the house and then only after spending an hour and a half walking UP HILL following paths made by the stranded cows.

Eagles Nest Ranch survived this storm with only the loss due to miscarriages while others in the state suffered a tremendous loss of 20,000 head of cattle. It was definitely a storm to be remembered.

Snow Shelters

To be better prepared, snow shelters were to be built. It had been planned before the 1997 blizzard with materials on hand but other projects had taken priority. This was a blessing in disguise because where we had first planned to build the shelters would have been in the wrong spots. All the needed materials were covered with snow. When all the snow in the pasture had melted, a new location was determined. The shelter in the east pasture would be placed where there would be additional natural protection from trees in the pasture to the north. Once again, the neighbors came to the rescue. A post hole digger that could dig a hole four foot deep was needed. The post that goes in this hole is 12' high so in order to build the shelter, the red pickup was put into service. The shelter is a semi-circle built from high poles, lumber and metal barn siding. Three 2x6's are connected horizontally onto the wood poles and then the barn siding is screwed to the lumber. We could not stand on a ladder while at the same time attaching the siding to the wood, so the back of the pickup was used as a work platform. Still a lot of stretching was needed, especially to reach the very top of the siding. The shelter is strategically placed so the back is in line with the predominate northwest wind direction. When there is a snow storm, the wind driving the snow will be stopped at the back of the snow shelter, forcing the snow to go around the shelter on either side. This leaves a clean spot in the shelter as well as a clear area in front. When hay is spread out for feed, it can be placed in this clear spot and the sheltered cows will be fed without having to walk in the snow. The cows know to go to the shelter and sometimes even calves are born there.

The third memorable storm is not about a huge storm or not being prepared but it concerns personal timing. The storm began on December 9, 1997 and continued to the 12th. There was not a huge amount of snow but the wind caused drifting, closing schools and highways. This story is about timing which began when our son, Tim called from Indianapolis saying a baby was to be born on the 15th. Grandma was needed to take care of granddaughter, Katie and I needed to be there by 5 p.m. on the 14th. The highways were now open and not a problem. The problem was the drift in the driveway, preventing me from getting to the house from the barn to get the necessary clothes and the car. Once again, a neighbor, Dwight Olkjer came to the rescue with his large tractor. He quickly dug through the drift and left saying, "Have a safe trip." I got to the house, loaded the car with clothes, blankets, food, candles and all other important necessities for winter driving. I left Elbert at three

Ruth building the much needed snow shelter with nosy cows watching the activity.

Snow shelter completed and ready for the next snow storm.

thirty in the afternoon, drove to Kansas, stopping for a quick night, up at four thirty, getting back on the road, arriving in Indiana at 5:30 p.m. Mother and father went to the hospital. Baby Michael was born during the night so all went well.

The cattle were all in Nebraska for "winter camp" so Grandpa flew to Indy and we all had Christmas together. How about that for timing?

Now, being weather channel addicts, we make sure when there is a storm approaching, all the cows/calves will be confined to the corrals by the barn and shed. Water is always available and hay is put in a hay ring which keeps it dry and off the ground. We are confident that everything is ready for any and all snow storms so BRING IT ON! The moisture is always needed!

Snow Fences

Long before we had purchased the land, snow fences had been strategically erected so as to keep the snow from drifting on to the main road. For those who have never experienced a snow fence, it is a series of thin wood stakes wired together set back from the road on pasture land. When the wind is driving snow, the snow will drift in behind the fence allowing only a small amount of snow to continue onto the road or into the pasture.

One day, after a big snow storm had more or less closed the main road because of drifting, I realized the original snow fence required fixing or even replacement.

I called the county Road and Bridge Supervisor and told him if he would bring out replacement fencing, we would install it. The answer was, "No, we can't do that." My thinking was that if the fencing could be fixed, it would make work easier for the people operating the snow plow. This was "woman's logic." A few weeks later, the

This living snow fence eliminated large drifts on the road.

Road and Bridge Supervisor called and asked me, "What would you think about having a living fence on your land?" I through it would be great."

The Colorado Living Snow Fence Program began in 1982 under the leadership of Dr. Dale Shaw, a retired forester from the Colorado State Forest Service. (USDA 2/21/17 Katherine Burst-Johnson). A living snow fence consists of trees and shrubs planted in rows parallel to roads, creating barriers which trap the wind-blown snow thereby preventing it from reaching the road. Not only do these fences help the ranches by providing necessary moisture, they also cut the maintenance time for road clearing. At the time of the year when trees could be successfully planted, two long lines of black plastic were laid on the ground and sapling cedar trees were planted through holes in the plastic. For the first few years, there was still snow behind the wood fences but slowly as the trees grew, more snow was caught, providing the necessary moisture for growth. This living fence also eliminated large drifts on the road. Smiling, may I say, "I told you so?"

EAGLES NEST AS A NATURE PRESERVE

While growing up in Cedar Rapids my family would often go to Beaver Park for summer picnics. Here we could observe a few wild animals living in pens in cement block structures which had openings where the animals could go for shelter. I remember how the animals, bears, foxes, and monkeys to name a few, would pace back and forth behind the high steel rod fences and the stench was horrible. Of course, I was young and a girl, so every bad smell was beyond belief!

Now as an adult, I have had the privilege of experiencing wildlife nature at its best in its natural habitat. When we lived at the Academy, we only had two species of birds that were easily seen, blackbirds and magpies. At the ranch we have so many different varieties. I keep the National Geographic bird book close at hand and make a note when a new species is sighted. I do miss the cardinals we had in Indiana but their beauty is replaced by that of the western tanager. We still have the blackbirds and magpies but they are in company with Steller's jays (named after German naturalist Georg Steller.) Although the eagles only visit occasionally, we still see hawks and falcons soaring through the beautiful blue sky as well as a couple of new species.

Have you ever been sitting alone in a room and felt as if you were being watched? I had this experience when all of a sudden, I could feel two great eyes staring at me. I was being observed by a great horned owl that was perched on a limb of the tall ponderosa pine tree just outside the window of the house. It was one of a pair of these beautiful birds that hang out in the shed by the barn. It is not unusual to hear them calling out during the night as they are nocturnal, but I had never seen one up close and personal. This owl has a bulky shaped body with a huge wing span of approximately four feet across which makes identification easy when they are spotted in flight.

The other new bird for me was the wild turkey, similar in size and color of a vulture that is definitely not a friend of the cattle. The vultures have been known to attack new born calves who are not yet mobile. This one spring day when a wild turkey appeared in our winter pasture, it created quite a reaction from the cattle. The cows were being fed hay from the large bales being spread on the ground behind the tractor. Usually the cows follow the tractor, trying to eat the hay as it is unrolled. On this day, I looked out the my "window on the world" and saw the cows and calves running as fast as they could, passing the tractor and the hay. This was MOST UNUSUAL! Off in the not so far distance was one wild turkey, not flying but running as fast as his legs could go, heading toward the nearest fence and possible safety. The cows/calves eventually gave up their chase, feeling they had done enough to scare the turkey away. They returned to the rolled-out hay and their meal for the day. The calves, although not old enough to be eating the hay, found some soft places to take a nap after their wild adventure.

The Variety of Wild Life

Not only do we have a variety of birds but we also have a great variety of wild life. As mentioned before, when we were first looking at this property, a group of

Twin mule deer fawns are just one part of the wildlife that share the ranch.

mule deer approached the truck in which we were riding. We had mule deer at the Academy and we would drive the perimeter road at dusk just to see how many we could find. Now we also have white tail deer who are tan colored with a distinct white tail. They are usually found closer to the available water found across the road near the creek. It is not unusual to see the mule deer, elk and pronghorns in the pastures with the cows.

Mule deer taking a rest outside our window.

The mule deer are probably the most prevalent and during hunting season seem to know they are safe here on the ranch.

We had one deer who spent a couple of days laying on our front yard just enjoying the soft green grass and certainly not in any hurry to go elsewhere. The hay bales stacked as steps provided a great play area for a few of the deer who decided to play "King of the Hill" as they climbed to the top. Art would yell, "Get off of there" but they would just look at him and continue eating. We know we are not supposed to feed the wild life but since the deer can move faster and jump higher, who are we to argue? We have many deer stories and all have happy endings. One evening we were sitting in our family room on the lower level of our house and it was dark outside so we had the lights and television on when all of a sudden, I looked out the glass doors and came face to face with six deer. We have an electric fence surrounding the grassy area behind the house but the deer had apparently jumped over it and now stood looking at their reflections in our doors. We were concerned that the deer might be thinking there were other deer instead of just their reflection, so we moved to the windows, hoping the deer would lose interest and walk away. Fortunately, this is exactly what happened so we and our windowed doors were safe.

My favorite deer story is one about a five-year-old boy, Trapper, and his father, Dan who were at the ranch to see the new born calves. Trapper had an older brother, Hunter, who had already found a trophy deer antler and had it hanging on his bedroom wall. Not to be outdone, Trapper needed one also. I had found an antler in the pasture a couple of days before and had put it over by a fence, sort of in plain view of little eyes. After they had seen the calves, I said to Trapper, "I think I saw an antler over by the fence. Let's go see if it is still there." Knowing full well it was, we started walking toward the fence. I was sort of hanging back so Trapper could find the trophy on his own. Mission accomplished! With a smile reaching from one ear to the other, Trapper ran back to his dad, "Daddy, Daddy, look what I found." The story does not stop here as when they were leaving, Dan, who happens to be an outfitter, looked out the truck window and spied another antler laying in the grass. He stopped the truck and said, "I think I might have seen something over there on the grass. Why don't you take a look?" Trapper jumped out of the truck, ran over and found a match of the first one he had found by the fence. What a day that had been for Trapper. He now had a pair of antlers to hang in his bedroom.

There is a herd of about seventy-five Elk that hang out along Kiowa Creek about three miles south of us. We have only occasionally seen a few here. We did see two yearling female elk in our winter pasture. As we watched, one jumped the fence while the other continued running back and forth along the fence, hoping to find an opening. Art opened one of the larger cattle gates and in time, the yearling saw it. She quickly joined the first one and they both took off across the road to Kiowa Creek. Since then, Greg saw about thirty-five elk crossing our northeast pasture. The elk are beautiful animals, larger and a darker tan than that of the mule deer and they also have the large white rump. Estes Park, Colorado has many elk which are seen quite often walking along the main thoroughfare of the town causing major traffic problems.

In addition to deer and elk, we also have pronghorn on the ranch grazing peacefully with the cattle. OK! What is a pronghorn?

The story goes (this may be only folklore) that when Lewis and Clark were preparing for their journey across the plains that they researched various species of animals. One of those was the antelope. When they got to the "high plains" of Colorado and Wyoming, they saw these hoofed animals, reddish-brown, tan or even darker brown in color with a large white rump. For Lewis and Clark, this species looked similar to an antelope so that is what they recorded. WRONG!

Whose land is this anyway? A calf and a pronghorn staring at each other in the pasture.

    Now I had never seen a pronghorn except at the Denver Museum of Nature and History and since they were on our land and we had to build our perimeter fence with the bottom wire, six inches above the ground so pronghorn could slide under it, I just had to know more. Pronghorn got their name from the horns on top of the heads. The female's horn is small, appearing as a lump while the male's horns are ten to twelve inches long. The horns have a unique shape in that they are straight at the beginning but curve later with the horns pointing backward to the rump. The name came because at the front of the horn is a small notch or prong pointing forward. Those on the ranch are tan, with white stripes on their necks, and have white markings on the face and stomach. They are about three feet tall, weighing between ninety and one hundred fifty pounds and are approximately four and one-half feet long. They have very long, but skinny legs which allows them to run at speeds close to 60 miles an hour, making them the fastest running creature in the United States. Their large eyes enable them to spot predators from very far away. They usually leave the ranch in September and return in late March or early April. When we had both pronghorns and the golden eagles on the ranch, there was a sad situation. Eagles were definitely a predator of the pronghorn and one day we saw an eagle carry away a baby pronghorn. Usually, when baby pronghorns are born, the mother will hide this extremely small offspring in the tall pasture grass. The mother will stand a way off but yet in a distance that provides a perfect line of slight. The eagle had spotted this baby and had it in its claws trying to fly back to the nest. The mother was chasing after the eagle but to no avail. Since the eagles are no longer on the ranch, it is a pleasure to see the little ones running, even faster than their mothers, across the pasture. The young will stay with their mother for about a year before becoming fully independent.

Apparently the pronghorn did not think our granddaughter, Katie, was a predator as she was out spraying weeds in the pasture, riding in the Gator with earphones blocking out all noises. All of a sudden, she felt a nudging at her elbow. She turned and found herself eye to eye with a pronghorn. Neither seemed to be afraid of the other so both went calmly about their business.

I got up and personal with a baby pronghorn one day while fixing fence but since I have already written about that in my fencing experiences, I will not repeat it except to say, I don't know who was frightened the most, me or the baby.

I am sure you have heard the expression, "Curiosity killed the cat" but here on the ranch the saying, "Curiosity means trouble for the cows." Cows are definitely curious creatures. One day Art and I were driving down our drive and off in the pasture was a group of cows with their heads to the ground. I said, "That looks weird." Art stopped the car. Looking over to the gathering, we saw a badger in the center of the cows, digging a hole as fast as he could. The cows, being curious as usual, were standing there watching. We got out of the car and I picked up a rock and threw it in the direction of the badger. This upset the critter who stopped digging long enough to sort of sit up and answer with a couple of funny sounds. "Pfsst, Pfsst" then immediately went back to digging. The cows finally lost interest, turned and walked away, leaving the badger to continue digging, thereby leaving a semi-large hole. I knew that Wisconsin was called the Badger State but I had never seen one so this was a first.

The danger of curiosity surrounding a porcupine is a serious problem for the cows and calves when they find themselves up close and personal with this critter. These nocturnal animals build nests in trees and in the winter will eat the bark off the trees causing the tree to eventually die. When the nosey cows or calves get curious about this funny creature roaming their territory and they get too close, the porcupine will release its quills which frequently land around the nose of the cow/calf or around their legs. The quills have barbs on them and when trapped under the hide of the cows are hard to remove. It is much like trying to get a sliver from a human hand. We have had to remove quills a few times. First, we spray the area with iodine and using tweezers, remove each quill one by one. If the quills surrounding the mussel of the cow are not removed, the cow will be unable to eat. So, it is best to remove the quills and not to wait for nature to take its course where eventually, the area will fester and the quills will fall out. Our "trapper friend" Dan is called on for help in the winter when porcupine tracks can be followed. He brings his trapping gear, and the porcupine who thinks he is safe in the culvert under the dam will be trapped and moved to a new location.

Two local bobcat kits catching a bit of sun on the ranch.

Curiosity is also normal in humans and so it was with me. Living in the country it is not unusual to have cats dropped off by people who just don't care enough to take on the job of raising a cat or dog. So, one day I was looking out the window in the front of the house when I saw what I thought was the tail of a cat. I didn't really think too much about it until the next day when I was looking out the bedroom window in the back of the house. I saw what I thought was an owl resting on a big rock. I called to Greg, "Come quick and bring your camera." The creature I was observing had large pointed ears, not huge but larger than those of a house cat and there was a lot of fur around the head. The color was sort of like an owl but there again, I had never really seen an owl "up close and personal." What a surprise it was when looking through binoculars, it was not an owl but a bobcat. I had never seen one before but Greg had, so I got a quick and informative nature lesson. We thought the cat had left the territory so was quite surprised when we saw not only a mother bobcat but her two kits walking down our drive, in front of the house.

There are many cave-like holes in some of the larger rock formations on the ranch, so just possibly our bobcat has a home there. We watched this mom as she sat near a drainage tube waiting for whatever critter was in the tube to come out. The kits got tired of waiting so they took off to do some exploring on their own but always returned to their mom. I was curious enough about this creature but not enough to go looking for her cave.

Human curiosity was once again aroused, not by me this time, but by Greg as he was in his bedroom one night and saw movement outside his window. He looked out and behold, there was a family of lynx including a male, female and kitten. Since lynx are not native to this area, Greg took a photo of them and reported the sighting to the U.S. Fish and Wildlife Service. They asked if the animals were tagged which they were not. This sighting occurred after Colorado had experienced forest fires so it is possible the animals had survived a fire and were looking for a new home. They have not been seen since but Greg's photo does prove the sighting.

This time it was not curiosity that killed the cat, it was a huge cat, a mountain lion who did the killing. As previously mention we check our cattle daily and one day, we could not find our six hundred pounds, six-month-old, red heifer. Many hours were spent searching and what we did find was only a partial carcass. Again the U. S. Fish and Wildlife Service was called. A representative came to the ranch and declared the heifer had been killed by a mountain lion. This was determined by the way the calf's neck was broken. We were told that mountain lions are territorial, operating in a ten-mile-wide radius. We truly hope this cat has moved onward and so far this tragedy has never been repeated.

Not wanting a good story go untold, I will tell you what I at first thought was a calf in a pasture by itself turned out to be a bear. Now, we knew bears had roamed the streets of Elbert. We had never seen one or the tracks of one until we were driving home from church and saw what I thought was a calf was really a bear. We watched as this bear came though the pasture and crossed the road behind us. Here is where we got curious, so we turned the car around and watched as this burly black creature disappear in a small grove of trees by the creek. We think it rather unlikely that a bear would visit us on the ranch as we are away from the creek, but we would never say "Never."

Cattle vs. the Unwanted

Do you know there are some animals that cattle do not want in their territories? If the truth be known, as ranchers, we don't want them here either but this is all part of nature. Take the prairie dog. Better yet, just take the prairie dog! Prairie dogs have taken over vacant fields and have become a real problem for humans when housing subdivisions are being built. I can't say for sure because I have never researched this topic but it seems to me, I can pass a vacant lot one day and see a few holes with the prairie dog standing by it and then a few days later, there will be many mounds of dirt with many, many more creatures running around there. For us, this animal is very destructive, leaving holes that all farm/ranch animals could accidentally step into, possibly breaking legs, forcing the demise of the animal. They also disturb the soil in the pasture, causing damage to the grasses that takes years to repair. When there are colonies of prairie dogs, the land becomes barren and cannot be used for pasture.

Another animal not really wanted is the Coyote. I think when we lived in Indiana, I saw maybe two coyotes at the most. Here it is not uncommon to see coyotes on the ranch during calving. Apparently, they watch cows giving birth and will try to get to the after birth if the cow/calf leave the spot before the cow has cleaned up the birthing area. Here we closely watch the cows during the day when they give birth. If a coyote should appear, the cow and calf will be quickly moved from any danger. It is likely that the coyotes are also giving birth at the same time as it is not unusual to hear their howling sounds, especially at night. The noise is usually quite loud but may be coming from some distance. If the windows are open and the sound is close, human action might well be taken. The danger from coyotes is if they are in a pack, they could and have been known to kill livestock. This has never happened here. Thank goodness.

Humans vs. Unwanted Creatures

There are some creatures here at the ranch which I have encountered only once or twice and hopefully will never see again. It was in the middle of June, shortly after moving from the barn to the house, when I was going to take the path through the trees and rocks to the barn. As I stepped off the last step from the deck, a skunk, very nonchalantly, walked across my desired path. I quickly and very quietly turned around, returning safely to the deck. That was the only time a skunk has been seen on the ranch, not saying there aren't more, but we can certainly do without them.

I can't say I enjoy seeing the little creepy, crawly creatures which invariably make me squeal, such as mice. While there is one species of mice that is supposedly endangered in Colorado, as far as I am concerned, all mice are in danger when they appear here at the ranch. Anything that is small and makes me squeal when movement is seen out of the corner of my eye is in danger of having a short life span. Mouse traps are set all over the house and in the barn. Mice seem to be especially busy when a seasonal change occurs and they are looking for a warm place to call home. I decided long ago that emptying mouse traps was not my calling so the job of clearing and refilling the traps with peanut butter is left entirely up to Art. He really doesn't like the job either but, "Oh well" that is what it is!

Another little creature here at the ranch is the so-called gophers. They are actually thirteen stripe ground squirrels. They are not a problem even though they dig tunnels and scurry around on the grass. Of course, if I see one moving quickly along and I am not expecting to see anything moving, I might give a slight "OOH" out of surprise and usually do!

Then there are the prairie lizards, a five-inch-long creature with various colors and patterns depending on the sex. Not knowing anything about this creature, I did some research and found it resides in open forests but also around country homes, of which we have both. I have been known to let out an "Eeeek" when this creature goes racing past. They move so fast even the fastest of little boys probably could not capture one. *The Discover Nature Field Guide* states that "this species commonly escapes capture by running up trees." When observed at the ranch, they are usually on the cement slab by the garage but close enough to trees to insure a safe departure.

Not to be overlooked are the red ants, who are interesting but wicked creatures. Since they are also one of God's creations, I will tolerate but will continue to give them their space. These ants build teepee shaped hills which are quite dangerous to people if one happens to step on it or accidently falls on one which I did. We were building a perimeter fence on a slope in the pasture and I lost my footing. I went sliding down the hill directly over the ant hill. I can't say if it was a bite or sting, but I could not get back to the house and into a shower quick enough. Although the hills are dangerous, they can also be informative. Supposedly, some people have found dinosaur teeth at the bases of the ant hills. How deep the ants dig is question for another day. Also, conservationists claim this digging by the ants is favorable to soil health. This I cannot confirm.

Humans and Preferred Animals

In addition to the not familiar animals, on the ranch we have also the more common variety of species. Red foxes are seen on the ranch but not often. Early on, it was not unusual for Art to look out his office window and see a beautiful fox walking in front of the house. There are a lot of rocks on the ranch that form sort of a cave, and as with the bobcats, a fox could possibly have a den there. It was truly a fun day when I was driving up the drive and what should appear were what I am sure were twin foxes, just walking down the drive, minding their own business. No fences or cement buildings here to hold these beautiful twins in confinement.

After a hard rain when there is a lot of water in the east winter pasture behind the dam, it is not uncommon to hear the croaking of frogs. I have never seen a frog here but I only go in the pasture when it is dry. I don't like to get muddy, that's the city girl in me! I wonder, where do the frogs go for a long period of time when there is no water behind the dam? For this, I have no answer!

Yes, we do have rabbits. We see their footprints during the winter. In the spring, when it is snowing, they take refuge under one of the many vehicles parked by the barn. They will also nest in among the hay bales and are so hidden, they are only exposed when the bale is removed. When the days are warm, the rabbits of all sizes may be seen scampering around the property, hopefully out of sight of the owls, hawks, or falcons.

Every once in a while, a lone Jack rabbit will be seen in the northwest pasture so a mystery remains of how he got here and where are the others, if there are any.

One of many rabbits enjoying Art's house plants on the porch.

Every now and then we realize a raccoon has been here, leaving tracks and possibly eating bird feed on the ground. One dark evening Art and I were sitting at the kitchen table, with the lights off watching TV. All of a sudden, I saw a dark figure walking on the railing of the deck. All I could say was, "What is that?" Art got up, turned on the outside lights and saw a raccoon climbing up the outside of the house. Where it went remains a mystery as it has not been seen since.

Every day on the ranch provides a new adventure or a new outlook on nature. This real-life story says it all. Art had put cracked corn on a tub for the squirrels to eat but what really happened is my favorite story. Picture this if you can. I looked out the glass door of my sewing room, only to see a six-point buck eating the corn. Just pass his nose, on the other side of the tub was a squirrel, sitting on his haunches. His tail was wagging and he was making a squeaky, chirping sound, as if scolding the deer. The deer just kept eating. Knowing he was not scaring the deer, the squirrel ran around the nearby juniper tree, returning only to find the deer still eating. Once again, the squirrel ran around the tree but still nothing had changed. The squirrel ran around the tree for the third time and this time he came up behind the deer and possibly thinking he could get to the corn by going between the legs of this huge obstacle. He stood there for a while and finally went back to the tree. Once the deer left, the squirrel took his turn at the corn. All the time this was happening, I was on the phone with my friend, Nancy, describing every bit of movement in front of me. She said, "Take a picture." My response was, "I can't. I think the deer would sense my movement and run off." So, for those of you trying to picture this story, it is the way it happened and aren't animals great?

How can I ever get lonely when I have all of God's creatures to keep an eye on? Watching the wild animals on the ranch is a wonderful experience and so educational. Our fences can either be jumped or flown over or crawled under. The animals are never confined, relocated, but not confined. They are free to find living spaces in caves or haystacks, under brush piles, or high in trees. There is no lasting odor, unless it is from a wandering skunk but that has never happened, at least not yet. We do not allow hunting on our ranch and it seems every fall, the deer take safe refuge here. What a wonderful place to view nature at its finest. I hope my stories have brightened your day and brought a smile to your face.

SAD DAYS AND GLAD DAYS

A sad day is always when a calf dies for whatever reason. As noted, many times, we watch our animals very closely so when a calf dies, we want to know why. My faith in God tells me it was nature's way but then I wonder how we might have prevented it, which, of course, is a human thought. The glad day is when a sick calf or cow has been treated, either by Art or the vet and the animal survives to become a viable part of the herd. We experienced bloating in calves and finally found a way to correct the problem if caught early enough. I couldn't do the fixing but I did help by mixing up the magic liquid solution given to the calf. The medicine has to be administered to the calf by using a stomach tube which must be safely and correctly inserted directly into the calf's stomach. The container holding the liquid must be held above the calf's head and must be squeezed quickly and hard to get it completely emptied. It definitely is a two-person operation and my part was to do the squeezing. It is more than just a "glad" day when we get to see the calf recover, it is a wonderful day!

Another sad day for me was when the load of our first steers went to market. I just could not go with them. They hadn't really become pets but they had been the first group of calves and we had watched them grow from birth. The next year we had both F1 heifers and steers to sell which meant going to two sales. I went along on both of these days still with sadness in my heart. I felt much better when the new owners of the heifers thanked us for having such docile animals, especially when they were to be around young children. The next years turned into "glad" years when previous buyers became repeat customers. Some had come to the sale just to buy our heifers but lost out because of higher bidders. The highest bidder went home happy. The losers said, "We'll be back next year. Hope you will be here also." One repeat buyer from Ogalallah, Nebraska had been sent to the sale by his son, who was busy with his daughter's soccer match. The father had asked his son, "What should I pay for them?" The son replied, "Just buy them!" He did and we delivered the calves to their new home. All parties were "glad."

A sad day is also when a first time heifer has a premature calf that doesn't survive. But a glad day is the next year when she has a female calf or even twins. One time there was a cow that had twins when Art had left for Nebraska for another load of cows. He had left early and I had gone back to bed. When I woke up and looked out the window into the corral, there was a cow with twins. It was very cold and I wanted to get them into the barn. I needed help so I called the Elbert Mini-mart. "Is there anyone there that could help me?" Kathy Phillips who worked there said, "If there isn't, I will find someone for you." It was not unusual for men to be sitting there having coffee so I was not surprised when within a few minutes, there were two men coming through the barn door. Unfortunately, we couldn't save but one calf who we got inside, got it warm and, thinking back, I think we got some honey into the baby. This calf survived. The men who helped me were Oliver Cook and Dwayne Royston and it was Dwayne that suggested the honey. (This was a treatment back in the dark ages.) The men even took the other twin away so I didn't have to see it on the ground leaving it for Art to bury. This was a sad day but it turned into a glad day. These two wonderful neighbors have remained friends all these years.

While there have been "sad" days, they are far outnumbered by the "glad" days. God takes care of all the animals and we are here to be His helper.

THE SHARING OF RANCH LIFE

Now that I have possibly learned all there is to learn about ranching, I realize the most important part of all is the ability to see and wonder about God's work. The beauty of the countryside after a fresh rain, the peacefulness of hearing birds singing or watching as they fly from tree to tree, the beautiful clean white snowflakes, seeing the various wildlife, the daily glances at Pikes Peak and being able to share all of this with family and friends.

I realized quite early in our ranching life that I was not only a ranch wife but also and activity chairwoman. Even before the cows had arrived and the house finished, we entertained the Western Sales District of ELANCO personnel in the barn. Of course, steak was on the menu and while I fixed the side dishes, Art did the grilling. Dinner was served on paper plates and since our table was only large enough for six people, our guests were sitting on benches balancing their food on their laps. It was a great evening!

Once the first calf arrived, our sharing of the ranch began in earnest. Art's mother, Sarah, was in her late 90s and had been raised on a farm. Her married life as farmer's wife was not easy as there was no electricity, no indoor water or plumbing and certainly no micro-wave to help in fixing a quick dinner. She never complained and her interest in farming/ranching never dwindled. When the first calf arrived at Eagles Nest Ranch, Sarah was the first to know. She wanted to know everything. What did the calf weigh, the sex of the calf, what was the coloring pattern and did the calf have the long eyelashes? All questions being answered, her comment would always be, "Land Sakes." There were times when she would be called three or four times a day but each call remained special even though the same questions were asked.

From describing and sharing each birth with Sarah, we realized, even more deeply, what a beautiful sight it was to observe the miracle of new life and even more so as we watched the cow caring for her new born. Art feels cows are the quintessential mothers and that no woman should have a baby without first watching a cow care for her calf.

Now, with cows on the ground, we could and were classified as ranchers. We were asked if we would be willing to entertain the members of the Colorado Purebred Angus Breeders as a stop on their field trip. As beginners, it was an honor and a great opportunity for us to get acquainted with Angus breeders. A local restaurant set up the barbecue where, needless to say, beef was the only meat served. This proved to be a wonderful experience and a good time was had by all.

The following December as Art was president of ARPAS (American Registry of Professional Animal Scientists), we served dinner to the Board of Directors and the people leading the Animal Science Board Certificates. Some were college professors and others were involved in various cattle industries. I was asked to join the group, so I sat quietly by and learn more about our bovine friends. It certainly was a beneficial evening for me.

We had already been sharing our ranch with friends but all of a sudden, we found that what we had been doing was just exactly what was needed. We were in attendance when Dr. Temple Grandin spoke to a group of Future Farmers of America. Some of you may recognize the name of Dr. Grandin as in 2010 she was pictured in a HBO movie, entitled, "Temple Grandin." She is a recognized Colorado State University Animal Behavior scientist who has developed the wildly used humane animal handling procedure. She told the audience that "The most important thing ranchers and farmers can do is to share ranch/farm life with city folk." WOW! We had already been doing that but now the idea was reinforced.

The sharing continued as the cows, even though large in size, seem to know when there are little children around. Our granddaughter Katie, who was about three years old, stood in the middle of a circle of cows. The cows were sure they would be given treats but first they were just observing this little creature standing upright on two legs and arms stretched out to touch the cows. There she was giggling and trying to hold the treat correctly in her hand so the cows could get to it. She got slobber all over her shirt, but the cows waited patiently, not one made an aggressive move toward this little human. It truly was a joy to watch. Could it be a motherly instinct?

There was another day when some grandparents brought their three-year-old grandson and his nine-month-old sister to the ranch. It was a beautiful summer day so the guests were put on the straw bales on the flatbed truck and out to the pasture we went. The grandson had seen cows across fences but never up close and personal. Of course, seeing the truck with people, the cows came running, expecting treats. The granddaughter looked across the field and all of a sudden, her first finger was sticking out in the direction of the oncoming cows. She was not old enough to really be talking but who needs to speak when finger pointing says it all? No one knows for sure what she was thinking but she was not frightened when the cows closed in on the truck. Her brother, being very brave at the old age of three, got off the truck with his grandfather so they both could give the cow treats.

Another great story of sharing was when three-year-old Jackson got to drive the tractor. He was sitting on Art's lap while operating the steering wheel which to him meant driving. When he got down from the seat, the smile on his face went from ear to ear. He asked his grandfather, Vern, "Did you see me drive?" This was only the first of many times for Jackson. As he grew older and taller, so did his driving experiences. The last time he drove was when he was in the driver's seat with Art standing of the ledge, riding shot-gun. Jackson is now a teenager without enough free time to visit the ranch. He has a little brother that hopefully will be able to visit and drive the tractor so the family tradition will continue. In between the two boys is a sister who is more interested in the calves than driving but all three enjoy coming to the ranch. We are more than happy to share it with them, making memories for all involved.

Greg loves to show the children the cows. He always asks them, "Do you know where your meat comes from?" The answer is always, "the grocery store." When Greg says, "No, it comes from animals like these." The children's eyes open wide in disbelief and they say "Really?" There was one time when someone asked, "Does chocolate milk come from brown cows?" Sharing of farms and ranches is very important.

Looking back over all the years that we have been ranching, we realize sharing was not a one-way street. Many professions have been represented by visitors. Artists have taken photos of the ranch and then transferred their work to canvass for all to see. Authors have written about the rock formations and the facts relating to the location. Educators, from teachers of pre-school children to college professors to university administrators have visited the ranch, including three teachers on an exchange from Bangkok, Thailand. Doctors, representing all facets of the medical profession and PhD's with various scientific degrees have shown an interest in the ranching operation especially the co-workers from Eli Lilly and ELANCO. They would ask Art, "Didn't you get enough of this when you had your forty hour a week job?" They certainly enjoyed the ranch as Art hosted a Bar-B-Que for an ELANCO reunion. Many others have asked, "Why did you choose this for a second occupation rather than just enjoying your retirement?" The answer was always, "It gives us a reason to get up every morning plus it gives us a purpose as well as providing needed physical exercise." There have been military personnel, some cadets from the United States Air Force Academy (one from Ecuador) and midshipmen from the United States Naval Academy, enlisted personnel and high-ranking retired officers. The military are usually asked "Where were you stationed?" If they were pilots they asked, "What plane did you fly?" There were many types of engineers, including "Domestic Engineers" commonly known as moms or wives who did not know how to change a light bulb or put air in a bicycle tire. All joking aside, there were engineers with degrees in relatively new fields. Some could share their occupations while others could not. There was even a couple with Australian shepherds who were training their dogs for Frisbee competition. A dairy farmer from Iowa was visiting and was watching me bringing the cows into the barn for treatment. He commented on how docile the cows were and he was sure his wife would not be doing what I was doing. Along the same line, there was a hog farmer from Leeds, England who was at the ranch with friends from Indiana. He was very impressed with the operation and insisted that we visit him so we could see how things were done in England.

How did we get acquainted these individuals? Some through relatives and/or friends who brought their friends along when visiting Colorado. Many came because of lasting military friendships and a great many were members of the Pathfinder class from the church. There were also foreign visitors including a friend from France who had been an exchange student while our family was living in Indiana. Another was a music teacher from London, who along with his family, had spent time in Colorado Springs teaching on an exchange basis. They loved Colorado so returned many times. It was such fun watching their twin girls grow during their yearly visits. An acquaintance that resulted in a lasting friendship was a family from Wales, Clive and Margaret Hare. I had stayed in their home while visiting Wales and had showed them on a map where I lived in Colorado. They had been to the states before but never to Colorado, so of course, they were invited to the ranch. Clive was sure he was meant to be a "Cowboy," so even though we did not have a horse for him to ride, he did enjoy the cows and calves. This resulted in many trips back and forth with many hours of sharing life experiences. Everyone has a story to tell, all that is needed is an audience to listen.

Have you ever shared a camp fire with a troop of Boy Scouts? After receiving permission from the local fire department, the ranch became a perfect site for a troop of scouts working on Astronomy, Orientation and Marksmanship badges. The boys and their leaders also enjoyed learning about the cows and calves even though there was no merit badge connected.

These are only a few of the stories of sharing, along with the annual Sunday School picnic, where the ranch is shared with many but all the money in the world cannot pay for these memories. I happily tell everyone that I have the best life ever. I love the ranch and am so very glad God gave both of us the opportunity for this wonderful experience. There was hard work, yes, but the rewards were beyond comprehension. When we are asked if we go to a gym to work out, we respond, "We are ranchers." We both remain physically fit and mentally alert as every day continues to be a learning experience. We enjoy the terrific sunsets and watching stars and the many planets through our telescope as there are no city lights to obscure the view.

Bring on the city folks, we are more than willing and happy to share.

SO WHY NOT, "WHY NOT?"

Over the years of ranching, I realize my "Why not" has opened my eyes to adventures and experiences I never dreamed I would be having. As a youth I helped plant gardens and pick various fruit from my grandfathers' trees but never thought about the "whys and wherefores." I was the oldest child of three and my father was gone a lot because of his employment so when the lawn needed mowing or the snow needed to be removed from the sidewalk, I learned how to do manual labor. It did not, however, include fence building or repairing one and it certainly did not prepare me for driving a truck pulling a trailer loaded with cattle. My "Why not" has shown me I can do almost anything and everything if I put my mind to it. One thing I still cannot do is make a dress without a pattern and I cannot draw a picture of a tree without making a note stating, "This is a tree!" But what I can do is put a hammer in my hand and attach staples to a fence post when building or repairing a fence and I can inform visitors about cross fencing and cross breeding and what a miracle it is when a calf is born.

When I am called to "go for" I don't have to worry about our dinner being spoiled if the fire under the kettle should go out. My life on the ranch is easy compare to that of Art's mother, Sarah who lived without electricity, indoor plumbing, tight windows during the Dust Bowl years, dish washers or a modern-day clothes washer and dryer. Heat for the house was marginal as there was no central heating nor air conditioning for the hot, humid Nebraska summer days.

Women throughout the ages have said, "Why not" and have been successful in fulfilling every challenge put to them. I am not the first "city girl" to become a rancher but I am part of a group of women who have also said, "Why not" and the many who will be following in years to come. There is absolutely nothing a woman cannot do if

Sunset at the ranch; may there be many more to share with others.

she puts her mind to it and in doing so, her unanticipated rewards will be great. I am so glad I said, "Why not" as I have loved every minute of my time on the ranch. There was hard work, yes, but the rewards were beyond comprehension. I have learned so much, not only about cattle but from the cattle. I know how to do wood working, how to make seat covers for all different vehicles and how to make an absolutely great meal on the spur of the moment for visitors.

We enjoy the terrific sunsets seen from the deck of the house and watching the many stars and planets through our telescope as there are no city lights to obscure the view. I am thankful for the God given opportunity to live with my husband, Art, on the ranch and to admire our accomplishments.

Would I go back to the city, NEVER!

www.ingramcontent.com/pod-product-compliance
Lightning Source LLC
Chambersburg PA
CBHW051549220426
43671CB00022B/2984